# Rita's
# Pocket PMP® Exam

By Rita Mulcahy, PMP

RMC
Publications, Inc.

ISBN: 1-932735-04-6
Library of Congress Control Number: 2005911003

Printed in the United States of America.

RMC Publications, Inc.
Phone: 952.846.4484
Fax: 952.846.4844
E-mail: info@rmcproject.com
Web: www.rmcproject.com

# Table of Contents

Introduction                                              *Page*

   How to Study Using This Book. . . . . . . . . . . . *v*

PMP Exam Simulation Questions

   Questions 1–200 . . . . . . . . . . . . . . . . . . . . . . . .*2*

Answers and Explanations

   Questions 1–200 . . . . . . . . . . . . . . . . . . . . . .*106*

Index: Questions by Process Group

   Initiating. . . . . . . . . . . . . . . . . . . . . . . . . . . . . .*174*

   Planning. . . . . . . . . . . . . . . . . . . . . . . . . . . . . .*175*

   Executing . . . . . . . . . . . . . . . . . . . . . . . . . . . . .*177*

   Monitoring & Controlling . . . . . . . . . . . . . .*179*

   Closing. . . . . . . . . . . . . . . . . . . . . . . . . . . . . . .*181*

   Professional Responsibility . . . . . . . . . . . . .*182*

# How to Study Using This Book

I suggest that you use this book AFTER you have studied the book *PMP® Exam Prep* and are ready for more difficult questions.

To be successful at answering the wordier questions on the exam, you must first interpret what topic the question is asking about and then determine what knowledge to apply.

Here is one of the tricks from the book *PMP® Exam Prep* for answering long, wordy questions:

1. Find the actual question in the data or situation.
2. Identify the topic being asked about (*schedule development, time, cost, conflict resolution, changes*) and any descriptors (*first, last, best, not, except*).
3. Read the entire question, ignoring any information not relevant to the question.
4. Come up with an answer.
5. Compare your answer to choice D and then C, B, and A until you discover the correct or "best" answer.

PLEASE NOTE: The questions contained in this book are a small subset of more than 1,400 questions on the PMP Simulation CD-ROM *FASTrack®*.

# Rita's
# Pocket PMP® Exam
## Questions

## Question 1 of 200:

Which type of organization is BEST for managing complex projects involving cross-disciplinary efforts?

- A. Projectized
- B. Functional
- C. Line
- D. Matrix

*(Answer, p 106)*

## Question 2 of 200:

A person you are working with has just passed the PMP exam. You are familiar with her experience, and you know she does not meet PMI's experience requirement for taking the PMP exam. What is the BEST thing to do?

- A. Contact your manager.
- B. Ask the person how she qualified.
- C. Contact PMI about the possible violation.
- D. Do nothing, as you do not know there is a problem.

*(Answer, p 106)*

## Question 3 of 200:

The engineering resource group, a matrixed organization of which a project manager's project team is a part, has a policy of no salary bonuses for project work. The project manager's current project has an aggressive timeline and a difficult technical obstacle to overcome. A new product offering is dependent on this project's success in the current timeline. The project manager has heard grumbling from his team members about the fact that they cannot be rewarded for their effort. What is the FIRST thing the project manager should do?

A. The project manager should determine whether other team members from another department can help with the project.

B. The project manager should talk to management to determine other rewards that can be given.

C. The project manager should negotiate a less aggressive schedule from the client.

D. The project manager should talk with the team about the importance of getting this done on time and explain the company policy.

*(Answer, p 106)*

## Question 4 of 200:

All of the following are part of administrative closure EXCEPT?

- A. Collection of records
- B. Analysis of project success and effectiveness
- C. Coordinating the operations and maintenance phase of the project
- D. Archiving project information

*(Answer, p 107)*

## Question 5 of 200:

The project is completed and the final deliverable has been sent to the customer, but the customer refuses to give final acceptance of the project. It is MOST important for the project manager to:

- A. inform management of the situation.
- B. ask the team for assistance.
- C. document the situation.
- D. initiate legal proceedings.

*(Answer, p 107)*

## Question 6 of 200:

You are a seller with unclear directions and scope documentation. Time and cost are important considerations, and the buyer wants to be in full control. What is the BEST contract to use?

A.  FP (Fixed price)
B.  T&M (Time and material)
C.  PO (Purchase order)
D.  CR (Cost reimbursable)

*(Answer, p 107)*

## Question 7 of 200:

A project manager is starting work on a complex project. There will be people from two different countries involved. The project sponsor is from a third country, and the work is being done on an expedited schedule in your country, with 14 electrical engineers, 4 architects and their staffs, 3 mechanical engineers, and 2 maintenance experts. What should the project manager do to make sure all of the work on this projected is identified?

A.  Create a clear management plan, and put it in writing.
B.  Create a WBS with input from all parties involved.
C.  Identify the laws of each country involved.
D.  Create a scope control system.

*(Answer, p 107)*

## Question 8 of 200:

A market demand, a business need, and/or legal requirements are examples of:

A.   reasons to hire a project manager.
B.   reasons projects are initiated.
C.   reasons people or businesses become stakeholders.
D.   reasons to sponsor a project.

*(Answer, p 108)*

## Question 9 of 200:

Halfway through the project, the client considers cancelling the remaining work and the contract. It would be BEST to look at which of the following to determine the purpose for the project?

A.   The project description and need in the project charter
B.   The WBS dictionary to verify that the scope is correct
C.   The risk response plan to evaluate alternatives
D.   The chart of accounts to determine the estimate at completion

*(Answer, p 108)*

## Question 10 of 200:

Negotiations between two parties are becoming complex, so party A makes some notes that both parties sign. However, when the work is being done, party B claims that they are not required to provide an item they both agreed to during negotiations, because it was not included in the subsequent contract. In this case, party B is:

- A. incorrect, because both parties must comply with what they agreed upon.
- B. correct, because there was an offer.
- C. generally correct, because both parties are only required to perform what is in the contract.
- D. generally incorrect, because all agreements must be upheld.

*(Answer, p 108)*

## Question 11 of 200:

You are the project manager for one part of a new program in your organization. You are four months into a three-year project when your project team makes significant discoveries on your project. What is the BEST thing to do?

A. Make certain the discoveries are included in the project lessons learned.

B. Make certain the discoveries are in the monthly status report.

C. Make certain you mention the discoveries at the senior management meeting in two months.

D. Make certain you tell the other project managers involved in this program about the discoveries at the weekly meeting.

*(Answer, p 108)*

## Question 12 of 200:

You are a project manager for a U.S. $3,000,000 product development project. Your project is well into the executing process group and remains on time, on budget, and on specification. This morning your project sponsor called to express concern about the project. Based on the schedule baseline, the project should be nearing implementation, but the sponsor does not know the current status of the project. You remind the sponsor that your team produces a detailed status report weekly and distributes it via e-mail. The sponsor indicates that e-mail is too impersonal and verbal updates are preferred. This situation suggests problems with which of the following project management processes?

- A. Communications planning
- B. Information distribution
- C. Performance reporting
- D. Stakeholder management

*(Answer, p 109)*

## Question 13 of 200:

A project team member is talking to another team member and complaining that so many people are asking him to do things. If he works in a functional organization, who has the power to give direction to the team member?

- A. The project manager
- B. The functional manager
- C. The team
- D. Tight matrix

*(Answer, p 109)*

## Question 14 of 200:

You are assigned as a project manager to lead a new quality improvement project. Management is asking for a project management plan. Which of the following should you create FIRST?

- A. A preliminary project scope statement
- B. A quality management plan
- C. A project management plan
- D. A project scope statement

*(Answer, p 109)*

A project may be selected based on all of the following EXCEPT?

   A.   Benefit measurement
   B.   Net present value (NPV)
   C.   The number of resources used
   D.   Value analysis

*(Answer, p 110)*

## Question 16 of 200:

Consideration of on-going operations and maintenance is crucially important to products of projects. On-going operations and maintenance should:

   A.   be included as activities to be performed during project closure.
   B.   have a separate phase in the project life cycle, because a large portion of life cycle costs is devoted to maintenance and operations.
   C.   not be viewed as part of a project. A project is temporary with a definite beginning and end.
   D.   be viewed as a separate project.

*(Answer, p 110)*

## Question 17 of 200:

Which of the following is an example of a tool used in quality planning?

   A.   Fishbone diagrams used to evaluate a defect
   B.   Quality audits
   C.   Control charts
   D.   Benchmarking

*(Answer, p 110)*

## Question 18 of 200:

Another project has had a major defect, and the project manager has gotten the project team and the process engineers involved in analyzing how this might affect their project. Which of the following would BEST describe what the group is involved in?

   A.   Quality analysis
   B.   Quality planning
   C.   Perform quality assurance
   D.   Perform quality control

*(Answer, p 111)*

## Question 19 of 200:

Your company has a policy that only a certain hotel chain may be used for business travel. You discover that a more expensive hotel is offering a discount on the days you need to be in town. What should you do?

A. Ask your manager for permission to use the other hotel chain.

B. Contact the hotel chain to negotiate a better rate.

C. Use the company's hotel chain.

D. Provide justification on your expense report for using the other hotel chain.

*(Answer, p 111)*

## Question 20 of 200:

A difference between the requirements is BEST resolved in favor of the:

A. sponsor.

B. project manager's boss.

C. stakeholder.

D. customer.

*(Answer, p 111)*

## Question 21 of 200:

Important aspects of a product include the on-going operations and maintenance. Which of the following BEST describes how operations and maintenance activities impact a project?

A.  They should be included as activities in the project WBS.

B.  Work involved in turning over the product of the project should be included as part of the project.

C.  They should be undertaken as separate projects under a mutual program.

D.  They should not be broken out as separate phases in the project life cycle.

*(Answer, p 112)*

## Question 22 of 200:

You have been working on a very large software development project that has made use of more than 230 people. Finally, all the scope has been completed. It would be BEST to:

A.  throw a party for the team members.

B.  make sure the project is integrated with other projects.

C.  begin to focus on your other projects.

D.  analyze project success or failure.

*(Answer, p 112)*

## Question 23 of 200:

Who determines the project scope requirements of a new project?

- A. The customer
- B. The stakeholders
- C. The project manager
- D. Senior management

*(Answer, p 113)*

## Question 24 of 200:

A project manager is trying to coordinate all the activities on the project and has determined the following: Activity 1 can start immediately and has an estimated duration of one week. Activity 2 can start after Activity 1 is completed and has an estimated duration of four weeks. Activity 3 can start after Activity 2 is completed and has an estimated duration of five weeks. Activity 4 can start after Activity 1 is completed and has an estimated duration of eight weeks. Both Activities 3 and 4 must be completed before the end of the project. If there is an approved change to Activity 4 and it now takes 10 weeks, what is the duration of the critical path?

- A. 10
- B. 11
- C. 14
- D. 8

*(Answer, p 113)*

## Question 25 of 200:

You have a firm fixed price (FP) contract with a clause stating that all changes to the contract statement of work must be written. One of your team members verbally instructed the seller to add a change that resulted in a 100 percent work package overrun. In this situation, what conflict management strategy should you use (as the project manager) with the team member?

A. Punishment
B. Problem solving
C. Negotiating
D. Withdrawal

*(Answer, p 113)*

## Question 26 of 200:

A company has just contracted with a well-known software developer to provide services during the planning and design phases of your project. Invoicing requirements were specifically defined within the contract, but limits on the seller's expenses were overlooked. As the project manager, what action should you take?

A. Modify the terms of the contract.
B. Define acceptable limits to be adhered to.
C. Proceed in good faith.
D. Terminate the contract.

*(Answer, p 114)*

## Question 27 of 200:

A project manager has very little project experience, but he has been assigned as the project manager of a new project. Because he will be working in a matrix organization to complete his project, he can expect communications to be:

  A.  simple.
  B.  open and accurate.
  C.  complex.
  D.  hard to automate.

*(Answer, p 114)*

## Question 28 of 200:

You are a project manager for a major information systems project when someone from the quality department comes to see you about beginning a quality audit of your project. The team, already under pressure to complete the project as soon as possible, objects to the audit. You should explain to the team that the purpose of a quality audit is:

  A.  part of an ISO 9000 investigation.
  B.  to check if the customer is following the quality process.
  C.  to identify inefficient and ineffective policies.
  D.  to check the accuracy of costs submitted by the team.

*(Answer, p 114)*

## Question 29 of 200:

According to your project network diagram, the critical path for the project is six weeks. One week into the project, the manager of the project management office informs you that the executive steering committee has moved the project's finish date to two weeks sooner than your published finish date. Assuming you are on schedule, what is the project float?

A.  Two weeks
B.  Four weeks
C.  Minus four weeks
D.  Minus two weeks

*(Answer, p 115)*


## Question 30 of 200:

A company and its seller are in the middle of a long dispute over the costs of terminating the contract. The project manager determines that the only way to resolve the problem is to have it heard and resolved by a neutral party. To accomplish this, the project manager should use a(n):

A.  functional resource manager.
B.  conflict solution expert.
C.  arbitrator.
D.  lawyer.

*(Answer, p 115)*

## Question 31 of 200:

During project planning in a matrix organization, the project manager determines that additional human resources are needed. From whom would he request these resources?

- A.   The project manager
- B.   The functional manager
- C.   The team
- D.   The project sponsor

*(Answer, p 115)*

## Question 32 of 200:

A watchlist is an output of which risk management process?

- A.   Risk response planning
- B.   Quantitative risk analysis
- C.   Qualitative risk analysis
- D.   Risk management planning

*(Answer, p 115)*

## Question 33 of 200:

A project has seven activities: A, B, C, D, E, F, and G. Activities A, B, and D can start anytime. Activity A takes three weeks, Activity B takes five weeks, and Activity D takes 11 weeks. Activities A and B must be completed before Activity C can start. Activity C takes six weeks. Activities B, C, and D must be completed before Activity E can start. Activity E takes two weeks. Activity F can start as soon as Activity C is completed and requires four weeks. Activity E must be completed before Activity G can start. Activity G takes three weeks. Activities F and G must be completed for the project to be completed. Which activities have float available?

- A. Activity A has two weeks float; Activity F has one week.
- B. Activity F has one week float.
- C. There is no float available in the project.
- D. Activity A has eight weeks float.

*(Answer, p 116)*

A seller is giving you so much trouble that your time available allocated to the project has gone from 20 percent to over 80 percent for this small piece of the overall project. Most of the seller's deliverables are late and inadequate, and you have little confidence in his company's ability to complete the project. What should you do?

A.  Terminate the seller for convenience, and hire another seller.

B.  Assign a group within your team to meet with the seller, and reassign project work so that the seller has easier work to accomplish.

C.  Meet with the seller to discover the cause of the problem.

D.  Provide some of your own staff to augment the seller's staff.

*(Answer, p 116)*

## Question 35 of 200:

On one of your company's medical research projects, you object to how the research is being handled. However, you signed a confidentiality agreement with the company that prohibits you from talking about your research. It would be BEST to:

- A.  quit and do not talk about what you know.
- B.  quit and begin talking to the community.
- C.  continue working and begin to talk about your objections to the research to newspapers in other cities.
- D.  destroy the research.

*(Answer, p 116)*

## Question 36 of 200:

The customer wants to expand the project scope after the project performance measurement baselines have been established. The customer will need to follow which procedures?

- A.  Scope control
- B.  Change control
- C.  Integrated management
- D.  Document control

*(Answer, p 117)*

The need for _____ is one of the major driving forces for communication in a project.

   A.   optimization
   B.   integrity
   C.   integration
   D.   differentiation

*(Answer, p 117)*

## Question 38 of 200:

A project has seven activities: A, B, C, D, E, F, and G. Activities A, B, and D can start anytime. Activity A takes three weeks, Activity B takes five weeks, and Activity D takes 11 weeks. Activities A and B must be completed before Activity C can start. Activity C requires six weeks to complete. Activities B, C, and D must be completed before Activity E can start. Activity E requires two weeks. Activity F takes four weeks and can start as soon as Activity C is completed. Activity E must be completed before Activity G starts. Activity G requires three weeks. Activities F and G must be completed for the project to be completed. What is the critical path?

   A.   Start–A–C–F–End
   B.   Start–B–C–E–G–End
   C.   Start–D–E–G–End
   D.   Both Start–B–C–E–G–End and Start–D–E–G– End

*(Answer, p 117)*

Which of the following statements represents a fixed price incentive fee (FPIF) contract?

- A. Pay $1,000,000.
- B. Pay all the costs plus $10,000 fee.
- C. Pay the costs plus $10,000 for every month the project is finished earlier than June 14.
- D. Pay $1,000,000 plus $10,000 for every designated incremental quality level reached.

*(Answer, p 117)*

The sponsor is worried about the seller deriving extra profit on the cost plus fixed fee (CPFF) contract. Each month the sponsor requires the project manager to submit CPI calculations and an analysis of the cost to complete. The project manager explains to the sponsor that extra profits should NOT be a worry on this project because?

- A. The team is making sure the seller does not cut scope.
- B. All costs invoiced are being audited.
- C. There can only be a maximum 10 percent increase if there is an unexpected cost overrun.
- D. The fee is only received by the seller when the project is completed.

*(Answer, p 118)*

The project has 13 team members and affects over 15 departments in the organization. Because the project is 20 percent complete to date and the team has had successful performance reports from five of the affected departments, the project manager holds a party to celebrate. The project manager invites to the party key stakeholders from all of the departments, in order to give those providing good reviews an informal opportunity to communicate good things to the departments that have not yet been affected by the project.

At the party, the project manager walks around to try to discover any relevant information that would help the project be more successful. He happens to hear a manager of one of the departments talking about setting up more regular meetings on the project.

The BEST thing for the project manager to do would be to FIRST:

A. record the effectiveness of the party in the project lessons learned.

B. review the information distribution methods on the project.

C. hold a meeting of all the stakeholders to discuss their concerns.

D. make sure the manager has a copy of the communications management plan so that he is reminded that such concerns should be sent to the project manager.

*(Answer, p 118)*

## Question 42 of 200:

The probabilistic analysis of the project is an input to which part of the risk management process?

  A.  Risk identification
  B.  Qualitative risk analysis
  C.  Quantitative risk analysis
  D.  Risk response planning

*(Answer, p 119)*

## Question 43 of 200:

While staffing a project in another country, the project leader from that country comes to you with a suggested team consisting of members of the project leader's family. Your FIRST course of action should be to:

  A.  inquire if hiring only through family lines is common practice in the project leader's country.
  B.  review the résumés of the individuals to see if they are qualified.
  C.  ask the project leader to provide additional names of people unrelated to him/her.
  D.  use a different project leader to prevent problems later in the project.

*(Answer, p 120)*

## Question 44 of 200:

The customer starts to have cash flow problems, because other projects are being completed early. The customer notifies the project manager that there will be limits on when funds will be available for the project. The project CPI is currently 1.02, and the estimate to complete is U.S. $927,000. If the project manager performs funding limit reconciliation, there will also MOST likely be a change to the:

- A. resources assigned.
- B. number of change requests.
- C. cost baseline.
- D. project schedule.

*(Answer, p 120)*

## Question 45 of 200:

Which planning output may be revised and refined as it moves through the procurement process?

- A. Contract changes
- B. Procurement documents
- C. The contract statement of work
- D. Proposals

*(Answer, p 120)*

## Question 46 of 200:

Which of the following is a basic rule or guideline for creating a work breakdown structure?

- A. The first row should describe the products of the project.
- B. Each level of a work breakdown structure is a smaller segment of the level above.
- C. A work breakdown structure should be like a to-do list, listing in chronological order every activity that needs to be done to complete the project.
- D. A work breakdown structure should be organized by functional areas.

*(Answer, p 121)*

## Question 47 of 200:

A new project manager is being mentored by a more experienced certified project management professional (PMP). The new project manager is finding it difficult to find enough time to manage the project because the product and project scope are being progressively elaborated. The PMP mentions that the basic tools of project management, such as a work breakdown structure, can be used during project executing to assist the project. For which of the following can a work breakdown structure be used?

- A. Communicating with the customer
- B. Showing calendar dates for each work package
- C. Showing the functional managers for each team member
- D. Showing the business need for the project

*(Answer, p 121)*

## Question 48 of 200:

What would be the BEST explanation for the following: Both the cost variance and schedule variance are negative, but the cost variance is lower than the schedule variance.

A.  The project underspent because all work was not completed but overspent for work that was done.
B.  The project overspent due to increased costs and yet completed some activities faster.
C.  The project activities took longer than expected, but costs were lower.
D.  The project underspent, because costs were lower than planned and activities were easier to complete than planned.

*(Answer, p 122)*

## Question 49 of 200:

As project manager of a project, you just handled a risk event that impacted the project cost and schedule. Because the impact is 15 percent of total project cost, what is the MOST appropriate action?

A.  Control the cost.
B.  Inform the appropriate stakeholders.
C.  Act to bring the cost of the event within acceptable limits.
D.  Update the project budget.

*(Answer, p 122)*

## Question 50 of 200:

All of the following are inputs to scope verification EXCEPT?

   A.   Work breakdown structure

   B.   Project scope statement

   C.   WBS dictionary

   D.   Project scope management plan

*(Answer, p 122)*

## Question 51 of 200:

If the optimistic estimate is one, the pessimistic estimate is nine, and the most likely estimate is eight, what is the PERT estimate?

   A.   9

   B.   7

   C.   8

   D.   3

*(Answer, p 123)*

## Question 52 of 200:

During the course of your project, you notice that most of the changes occurring on the project come from the research department. What should you do?

- A. Assign a team member to work solely with the research department.
- B. Change your communications management plan, so only you are assigned to interact with the research department.
- C. Ask the research department to assign one person to be your liaison.
- D. Talk to the research department to understand the reasons for the changes.

*(Answer, p 123)*

## Question 53 of 200:

The project manager is involved with schedule development for the project. She has analyzed the project, compressed the schedule and completed a Monte Carlo analysis. Which of the following is an output of schedule development?

- A. Activity duration estimates
- B. Recommended corrective actions
- C. Resource requirement updates
- D. Work breakdown structure

*(Answer, p 123)*

## Question 54 of 200:

A project team has been arguing for days about the correct way to complete a high-level design. This argument has caused the schedule performance index (SPI) to fall to 0.89 and the cost performance index (CPI) to 0.8. If the project manager tells the team, "we will schedule this discussion for our team meeting next week," the project manager is:

A. using earned value.
B. compromising.
C. increasing costs even further.
D. withdrawing.

*(Answer, p 123)*

## Question 55 of 200:

A rough order of magnitude estimate is made during which project management process group?

A. Project planning
B. Project closing
C. Project executing
D. Project initiating

*(Answer, p 124)*

Performance reports should address all the needs of:
- A.   management.
- B.   team members.
- C.   the project manager.
- D.   stakeholders.

*(Answer, p 124)*

A team member who does not have the required skills or knowledge was assigned to a team. Who is responsible for ensuring that he receives the proper training?
- A.   The sponsor
- B.   The functional manager
- C.   The project manager
- D.   The training coordinator

*(Answer, p 124)*

A control chart shows seven data points in a row on one side of the mean. What should be done?
- A.   Perform a design of experiments.
- B.   Adjust the chart to reflect the new mean.
- C.   Find an assignable cause.
- D.   Nothing. This is the rule of seven and can be ignored.

*(Answer, p 124)*

## Question 59 of 200:

An activity has an early start (ES) of Day 3, a late start (LS) of Day 13, an early finish (EF) of Day 9, and a late finish (LF) of Day 19. The activity:

A.  is on the critical path.
B.  has a lag.
C.  is progressing well.
D.  is not on the critical path.

*(Answer, p 125)*

## Question 60 of 200:

The first phase of your project has come to an end. What should you ensure is done BEFORE beginning the next phase?

A.  Verify that the resources are available for the next phase.
B.  Check the project's progress compared to its baselines.
C.  Confirm that the phase has reached its objectives, and formally accept its deliverables.
D.  Recommend corrective action to bring project results in line with project expectations.

*(Answer, p 125)*

A team member comes to you to tell you that there is a problem on her activity. It cannot be started on the day it is scheduled to start. A manager overhears this conversation and reports that the project will be late. Later the project manager completes his own report saying "the project is still scheduled to be completed on time." Which of the following could be the reason the project manager made such a statement?

A. The activity has free float and can be rescheduled later in its early-start-to-late-finish window.

B. The activity is on a near-critical path with less float than the length of the delay.

C. The activity is on the critical path but is to be done after another activity that does have float.

D. The activity has a mandatory dependency allowing the project manager to place it in the project schedule at any location that he wants it to be done.

*(Answer, p 125)*

## Question 62 of 200:

In which project management process group is the detailed project budget created?

A. Initiating
B. Before the project management process
C. Planning
D. Executing

*(Answer, p 126)*

## Question 63 of 200:

The financial systems project has a relatively high profile in the organization and has received great support from the sponsor. There are more than 230 activities on the project, and a few have remained relatively large due to the nature of the work to be accomplished. One of these larger activities has an estimate to complete that is longer than planned. If the project manager wants to look at nonvalue-added activities that might be causing the delay, the manager should:

A. measure using quality metrics.
B. complete process analysis.
C. perform a quality audit.
D. use a Pareto chart.

*(Answer, p 126)*

The code development phase of a software project is nearly complete when the first code review is conducted. During the review, it is discovered that the application is missing functionality required to complete a key business process. However, the product scope never specified this functionality. What should the project manager do?

A. Reject the functionality as out of the project's scope.

B. Agree to include the functionality in the current release.

C. Agree to include the functionality in the next release.

D. Assess the impact on the project of including the functionality, and inform the sponsor.

*(Answer, p 126)*

**Question 65 of 200:**

A project manager has put in place rules covering who will have access to controlled documents, how changes to these items will be recorded and approved, and how everyone will know what the current version is. The project manager is therefore creating a:

A. work authorization system.

B. change control system.

C. configuration management system.

D. project management information system.

*(Answer, p 126)*

## Question 66 of 200:

Who of the following are ALWAYS stakeholders?

- A. A person who does not want the project to be completed.
- B. An assembly line worker that will use the product of the project.
- C. A functional manager from the engineering department.
- D. A person who might lose their position in the company because of the project.

*(Answer, p 127)*

## Question 67 of 200:

You are having difficulty estimating the cost of a project. Which of the following BEST describes the most probable cause of your difficulty?

- A. Inadequate scope definition
- B. Unavailability of desired resources
- C. Lack of historical records from previous projects
- D. Lack of company processes

*(Answer, p 127)*

## Question 68 of 200:

All of the following are outputs of qualitative risk analysis EXCEPT:

- A. root causes of risk.
- B. probabilities and impacts.
- C. risk categorization.
- D. risk urgency.

*(Answer, p 127)*

## Question 69 of 200:

A company is attempting to select the BEST project from a list of possible choices. If the information they have includes the following benefit cost ratios, which project should they pick?

A.   2.2
B.   1.3
C.   0.8
D.   1.6

*(Answer, p 128)*

## Question 70 of 200:

During project executing, a project manager from the information systems department is trying to complete the project yet is constantly faced with interference from the manager of the engineering department. The engineering department keeps changing the resources assigned to the project team and its availability. What type of matrix does this represent?

A.   Strong matrix
B.   Weak matrix
C.   Functional matrix
D.   Tight matrix

*(Answer, p 128)*

## Question 71 of 200:

During the select sellers process of procurement, your objective is to obtain the best price possible. The tool that you will MOST heavily rely upon will be a(n):

- A. weighting system.
- B. screening system.
- C. independent estimate.
- D. part performance history.

*(Answer, p 128)*

## Question 72 of 200:

A project team is scattered across North America, South America, and Europe. There are seven companies working on the project and 67 core team members. Which of the following would have the GREATEST impact on making the situation easier to manage?

- A. Preliminary project scope statement
- B. A staffing management plan
- C. A change control system
- D. More time spent in scope planning

*(Answer, p 128)*

The project life cycle differs from the product life cycle in that the project life cycle:

    A.    does not incorporate a methodology.

    B.    is different for each industry.

    C.    can spawn many projects.

    D.    describes project management activities.

*(Answer, p 129)*

Three items from the issue log have been assigned to a team member. However, no action has been taken by the agreed-upon due date. After three calls to the team member, the work is finally completed. Which of the following is the BEST preventive action to take NOW?

    A.    Remove the team member from the team if possible.

    B.    Meet with the team member to uncover the reasons why there were problems.

    C.    Make sure the action item list is distributed to all the right parties.

    D.    Make sure items assigned in the action item list are accepted by the team members they are assigned to.

*(Answer, p 129)*

## Question 75 of 200:

A contract has just been signed with a construction company to complete a remodeling project within three months. Due to force majeure, the project will be delayed by an additional three months. However, the construction company does not have enough resources to complete the project and has asked for an early termination of the contract. What is the MOST appropriate thing to do in this situation?

- A. Bring details of the situation to the legal department.
- B. Complete administrative closure.
- C. Complete contract closure.
- D. Issue a change order for an extension of time.

*(Answer, p 130)*

## Question 76 of 200:

Your customer has asked for a 2,000-call capacity for the new call center project. However, one of your company's technical experts believes a 3,000-call capacity can be reached. Another thinks that based on the technical needs of the customer, the capacity needs to be only 1,500 calls. What is the BEST thing to do?

- A. Meet with the customer to better understand the reasons behind the 2,000 call capacity.
- B. Set the objective at 3,000 calls.
- C. Meet with the technical experts and help them to agree on an objective.
- D. Set the objective at 2,000 calls.

*(Answer, p 130)*

During project executing, you discover that you are working on work requested by the customer but not included in the contract. During previous meetings, the customer already spoke of being upset about the cost of several items she claims your company left out of the contract. No one in your company wants to discuss the change with the customer for fear of losing the contract. What is the BEST long-term course of action for the company?

A. Have a meeting with the customer to identify all the items she thinks were left out of the contract.

B. Contact your senior management and contract department to determine the options. Then schedule a meeting with management and the customer to discuss these options.

C. Look for ways to save time on other work packages so the new work can be done.

D. Renegotiate a new contract statement of work and a new contract.

*(Answer, p 130)*

## Question 78 of 200:

Which of the following is the BEST method to make reward systems MOST effective?

   A.   Pay a large salary increase to the best workers.

   B.   Give the team a choice of rewards.

   C.   Make the link between performance and reward clear.

   D.   Present notification of rewards within the company.

*(Answer, p 131)*

## Question 79 of 200:

A project manager overhears a conversation between two stakeholders who are talking about how unhappy they are with the impacts of the project on their own departments. Stakeholder A asks if the project is on time and Stakeholder B replies that the SPI is 1.05. Stakeholder A asks if the project manager for the project knows of Stakeholder B's concern. Stakeholder B responds that he is not sure. What is the BEST thing for the project manager to do?

   A.   Make sure the stakeholders see that the project manager overheard. Then ask them to direct any questions to the project manager in writing.

   B.   Make a presentation to all the stakeholders regarding the status of the project.

   C.   Send both stakeholders a copy of the issue log and ask for additional comments.

   D.   Arrange a meeting with both stakeholders to allow them to voice any concerns they may have.

*(Answer, p 132)*

## Question 80 of 200:

The project was going well until the director of marketing discovered that two of her staff members were working on different versions of the sampling plan, a product of your project. Which of the following BEST describes what needs the attention of the project manager on this project?

- A. Stakeholder management
- B. Resource allocation
- C. Staffing management plan
- D. Configuration management

*(Answer, p 132)*

## Question 81 of 200:

A project manager is managing a fixed price (FP) contract. She thinks that a large customer-requested change might impact the schedule of the project. What should she do FIRST?

- A. Meet with the stakeholders.
- B. Meet with the team.
- C. Renegotiate the remainder of the contract.
- D. Follow the change control system.

*(Answer, p 133)*

## Question 82 of 200:

Which motivational theory uses the concept of Theory X?

- A. Maslow
- B. Deming
- C. McGregor
- D. Herzberg

*(Answer, p 133)*

## Question 83 of 200:
Which of the following sequences represents straight line depreciation?

A. $100, $100, $100
B. $100, $120, $140
C. $100, $120, $160
D. $160, $140, $120

*(Answer, p 133)*

## Question 84 of 200:
A manager has responsibility for a project that has the support of a senior manager. From the beginning, you have disagreed with the manager as to how the project should proceed and what the deliverables should be. You and he have disagreed over many issues in the past. Your department has been tasked with providing some key work packages for the project. What should you do?

A. Provide the manager with what he needs.
B. Inform your manager of your concerns to get his support.
C. Sit down with the manager at the beginning of the project, attempt to describe why you object to the project, and discover a way to solve the problem.
D. Ask to be removed from the project.

*(Answer, p 133)*

## Question 85 of 200:

A project manager is trying to complete a software development project but cannot get enough attention for the project. Resources are focused on completing process-related work, and the project manager has little authority to properly assign resources. What form of organization must the project manager be working in?

- A. Functional
- B. Matrix
- C. Expediter
- D. Coordinator

*(Answer, p 134)*

## Question 86 of 200:

A project manager has a very large project budget, but the team lacks experience and adequate management support. Under these circumstances, what is the MOST effective way to get the work completed?

- A. Provide bonuses for meeting specific quality measures.
- B. Inform the team members that they will be fired if they do not perform.
- C. Spend some of the project budget taking the team members' bosses to lunch, and discuss the benefits of the project.
- D. Inform the team that they do not need to worry, because the project manager will provide the technical expertise.

*(Answer, p 134)*

## Question 87 of 200:

The product manager for the product the project is developing notifies the project manager that he has decided the product should be able to be used by an additional market. The BEST thing for the project manager to do would be to:

- A. immediately notify the project sponsor that there is a project scope change.
- B. notify the project change control board that the project scope will have to change.
- C. inform the product manager that the potential impact to the components of the "triple constraint" will be reviewed.
- D. do nothing, as this is an example of progressive elaboration.

*(Answer, p 135)*

## Question 88 of 200:

You are the project manager for a large installation project when you realize that there are more than 200 potential stakeholders on the project. Which of the following would be the BEST course of action for you to take?

- A. Eliminate some stakeholders.
- B. Contact your manager, and ask which stakeholders are most important.
- C. Gather the needs of all the most influential stakeholders.
- D. Find an effective way to gather the needs of all stakeholders.

*(Answer, p 135)*

## Question 89 of 200:

Quality on your project must be as high as possible, yet this type of project is new for your company. Which of the following is the BEST thing to do?

A.  Audit work as it is being completed to look for any improvements.

B.  Improve your work authorization system.

C.  Use cause and effect diagrams when there is a defect.

D.  Make sure your staffing management plan is up to date.

*(Answer, p 135)*

## Question 90 of 200:

In managing project communications, what should the project manager keep in mind?

A.  Communication skills are most important during project executing.

B.  The receiver is responsible for making sure communications are clear.

C.  Only the team members need to be concerned about communicating with each other.

D.  A choice must be made about how to communicate properly.

*(Answer, p 136)*

The seller tells you that your activities have resulted in an increase in their costs. You should:

   A.    recommend a change to the project costs.

   B.    have a meeting with management to find out what to do.

   C.    ask the seller for supporting information.

   D.    deny any wrongdoing.

*(Answer, p 136)*


**Question 92 of 200:**

You are managing the project when you discover an estimated completion date will occur after the desired date. What should you do FIRST?

   A.    Add resources to the project.

   B.    Evaluate the possibility of doing more activities in parallel.

   C.    Negotiate for more time.

   D.    Explain to the customer that the project cannot be done on time.

*(Answer, p 136)*

You have just been assigned as the project manager for a project that is in the middle of the executing phase, and you are determining how you will control the project. The BEST way to control the project is to:

A. use a combination of communication methods.
B. hold status meetings, because they have worked best for you in the past.
C. refer to the bar chart weekly.
D. meet with management regularly.

*(Answer, p 137)*

During project executing, a large number of changes are made to the project. The project manager should:

A. wait until all changes are known and print out a new schedule.
B. make approved changes as needed but retain the schedule baseline.
C. make only the changes approved by management.
D. talk to management before any changes are made.

*(Answer, p 137)*

**Question 95 of 200:**

A project manager has been overwhelmed with problems on his project. He would like to identify the root cause of the problems in order to determine where to focus his attention. Which of the following tools would be BEST for the project manager to use?

  A.  Pareto chart
  B.  Conflict resolution techniques
  C.  Fishbone diagram
  D.  Trend analysis

*(Answer, p 137)*

**Question 96 of 200:**

When a project manager is engaged in negotiations, nonverbal communication skills are of:

  A.  little importance.
  B.  major importance.
  C.  importance only when cost and schedule objectives are involved.
  D.  importance only to ensure you win the negotiation.

*(Answer, p 138)*

During project executing, a team member comes to the project manager because she is not sure what work she needs to accomplish on the project. Which of the following documents contain detailed descriptions of work packages?

A.  Work breakdown structure (WBS) dictionary
B.  Activity list
C.  Preliminary project scope statement
D.  Project scope management plan

*(Answer, p 138)*

A project manager is identifying the quality standards relevant to the project and determining how to meet them. This activity is:

A.  quality management.
B.  perform quality assurance.
C.  quality planning.
D.  perform quality control.

*(Answer, p 138)*

## Question 99 of 200:

Project Team A has been hired to manage a transportation project very similar to dozens of projects the team has managed successfully in the past. The team has determined that the probability of achieving project objectives is 94 percent. What part of the risk process is the team in?

- A. Qualitative risk analysis
- B. Risk response planning
- C. Quantitative risk analysis
- D. Risk identification

*(Answer, p 139)*

## Question 100 of 200:

A team member comes to you (the project manager) privately and informs you that an employee of your customer is making unwelcome advances. The team member has repeatedly requested that this person stop, but the advances continue. What is the BEST course of action?

- A. Privately confront the customer employee and threaten legal action if the advances do not stop.
- B. Suggest that the team member avoid contact with the customer employee.
- C. Contact the employee's manager to arrange a meeting to discuss the matter.
- D. Facilitate a meeting with the team member, the customer employee, and yourself to allow the two to work it out amicably.

*(Answer, p 139)*

## Question 101 of 200:

Which of the following would be the MOST appropriate thing to do during the planning process group?

A. Determine high-level stakeholders.

B. Hold a meeting with all stakeholders to make sure everyone is on the same page.

C. Implement approved process improvements.

D. Focus on preventing problems rather than dealing with them as they arise.

*(Answer, p 139)*

## Question 102 of 200:

You are assigned as the project manager in the middle of the project. The project is within the baselines, but the customer is not happy with the performance of the project. What is the FIRST thing you should do?

A. Discuss it with the project team.

B. Recalculate baselines.

C. Renegotiate the contract.

D. Meet with the customer.

*(Answer, p 140)*

## Question 103 of 200:

All of the following are required to bring a project to closure EXCEPT?

A.   Perform project feedback with the team.
B.   Obtain sign-off from the customer.
C.   Review project documentation for completeness.
D.   Update the project management plan.

*(Answer, p 140)*

## Question 104 of 200:

The MOST common causes of conflict on a project are schedules, project priorities, and:

A.   personalities.
B.   resources.
C.   cost.
D.   management.

*(Answer, p 140)*

## Question 105 of 200:

A team of seven people adds two more people to the team. How many communication channels are there now?

A.   9
B.   36
C.   18
D.   81

*(Answer, p 141)*

Work on a project is ongoing when the project manager overhears two workers arguing over what a set of instructions means. The project manager investigates and discovers that the instructions for the construction of the concrete footings currently being poured were poorly translated between the different languages in use on the project. Which of the following is the BEST thing for the project manager to do FIRST?

- A. Get the instructions translated by a more experienced party.
- B. Look for quality impacts of the poor translation of the instructions for the footings.
- C. Bring the issue to the attention of the team, and ask them to look for other translation problems.
- D. Inform the sponsor of the problem in the next project report.

*(Answer, p 141)*

How does MOST communication occur?

- A. Nonverbally
- B. Verbally
- C. Paralingually
- D. Referentially

*(Answer, p 141)*

## Question 108 of 200:

During the execution of your project, the seller loses key personnel who were working on your project. What is generally the BEST thing for a project manager to do in this situation?

A. Remind the seller of the next delivery due date.
B. Contact the other bidding vendors, and see if one could complete the project.
C. Work closely with the seller to review the qualifications of any replacement staff.
D. Attempt to hire the people to work directly for you.

*(Answer, p 142)*

## Question 109 of 200:

Total float is the amount of time an activity can be delayed without delaying the:

A. project.
B. completion date required by the customer.
C. early start of its successor.
D. project completion date.

*(Answer, p 142)*

A person who has been working as a project expeditor for the past three years has just been named as project manager for a construction project in a neighboring state. The construction crew has worked together for a number of years. One of the project manager's responsibilities is to pursue all of the historical risk information available, but he doesn't have enough time to access all available sources. The project manager would be best served by relying LEAST on which of these sources?

- A. Project files
- B. Published benchmarking reports
- C. Project team knowledge
- D. Lessons learned databases

*(Answer, p 142)*

The project manager has a project that is three months behind but, surprisingly, markedly under budget. She has decided to try to make up time, but needs to minimize the project risk. What is the BEST thing to do?

- A. Crash
- B. Fast track
- C. Redefine the scope
- D. Resource level

*(Answer, p 142)*

## Question 112 of 200:

Senior management asks the project manager how the project would be affected if two resources were removed from the project. To calculate a response, the project manager should complete:

- A. resource leveling.
- B. what-if scenario analysis.
- C. schedule compression.
- D. fast tracking.

*(Answer, p 143)*

## Question 113 of 200:

A project manager's scope management efforts are being audited. The cost performance index (CPI) on the project is 1.13 and the benefit cost ratio (BCR) is 1.2. The project scope was created by the team and stakeholders. Requirements on the project have been changing throughout the project. No matter what the project manager has tried to accomplish in managing the project, which of the following is he MOST likely to face in the future?

- A. Having to cut costs on the project and increase benefits
- B. Making sure the customer approved the project scope
- C. Not being able to measure completion of the product of the project
- D. Having to add resources to the project

*(Answer, p 143)*

## Question 114 of 200:

Project reports are a method to:
- A.   plan communications.
- B.   distribute information.
- C.   report performance.
- D.   manage resources.

*(Answer, p 144)*

## Question 115 of 200:

Which of the following BEST describes a project management plan?
- A.   The schedule, management plans, and budget
- B.   The project manager's plan for managing and controlling the work
- C.   The project charter, WBS, and project scope statement
- D.   A formal, approved document used to control the project

*(Answer, p 144)*

## Question 116 of 200:

What leadership style should you employ during the first two weeks of project planning?
- A.   Coaching
- B.   Directing
- C.   Supporting
- D.   Facilitating

*(Answer, p 144)*

## Question 117 of 200:

The management theory that states all people can direct their own efforts is:

- A. Theory Y
- B. Herzberg's theory
- C. Maslow's hierarchy
- D. Theory X

*(Answer, p 144)*

## Question 118 of 200:

All of the following are purposes of the project charter EXCEPT?

- A. It establishes the project.
- B. It identifies the product acceptance criteria.
- C. It gives the project manager authority.
- D. It includes stakeholders' requirements.

*(Answer, p 145)*

## Question 119 of 200:

Which of the following is the BEST tool for showing the team the project schedule status during project executing?

- A. Milestone chart
- B. Bar chart
- C. Work breakdown structure
- D. Network diagram

*(Answer, p 145)*

## Question 120 of 200:

A project team is having difficulty communicating over long distances. There were 13 team members from two countries, and then five people from India were added. This is of concern to the project manager because:

A.    communications grow exponentially.

B.    it will be harder to use reward power.

C.    communication blockers grow linearly.

D.    conflict can be increased with an increase in project priorities.

*(Answer, p 145)*

## Question 121 of 200:

The project manager wishes to use the Delphi Technique to obtain expert opinion on some difficult technical issues she's facing. What should she be careful to do?

A.    Make sure the experts consulted are recognized for their input.

B.    Compare information and work toward a single opinion.

C.    Consult the stakeholders.

D.    Meet together with the experts to obtain consensus.

*(Answer, p 145)*

## Question 122 of 200:

During the planning processes, activity G was estimated to take five days. Activity G is on the critical path. On day 2, it becomes clear that activity G will take 15 days, which will impact the imposed project end date. The project team meets to perform root cause analysis to identify the cause of the variance and to plan schedule recovery with activities performed later in the schedule. Which of the following should ALWAYS be the output of this kind of meeting?

- A. Recommended corrective action
- B. WBS updates
- C. Activity list updates
- D. Schedule updates

*(Answer, p 146)*

## Question 123 of 200:

During risk monitoring and control, the risk response owner should be:

- A. identifying which risks he/she wants to monitor.
- B. controlling the identification of response strategies.
- C. informing the project manager of any midcourse correction needed.
- D. updating stakeholders of new strategies for mitigating risks.

*(Answer, p 146)*

## Question 124 of 200:

Which of the following is the WORST way to resolve conflict?

- A. Compromising
- B. Forcing
- C. Smoothing
- D. Withdrawal

*(Answer, p 146)*

## Question 125 of 200:

During the identification of risks on your project, you have determined that there is a very high probability of conflict among the stakeholders during project executing over one aspect of the final design of the project. Which of the following is an example of mitigating the impact of the risk to the project?

- A. Obtain an insurance policy for the anticipated cost of the impact.
- B. Provide the team with training on conflict resolution techniques.
- C. Outsource that part of the project to another company.
- D. Eliminate that part of the project.

*(Answer, p 147)*

## Question 126 of 200:

All of the following are outputs of the Create a WBS process EXCEPT?

A. Scope baseline
B. Requested changes
C. Recommended corrective actions
D. Updates to the project scope statement

*(Answer, p 147)*

## Question 127 of 200:

A project manager is working on a major new product development project when a risk occurs that does not have a risk response plan. What should the project manager do?

A. Hold a risk reassessment, and plan a workaround.
B. Inform management, and communicate the new risk to the team.
C. Communicate the planned response to the stakeholders.
D. Use some of the reserves to accommodate the risk.

*(Answer, p 147)*

## Question 128 of 200:

You are managing a two-year project involving staff from several departments. The project is on schedule and within budget. A key team member leaves for a four-week vacation without completing a highly technical and specialized activity assigned to her (activity A). The project team cannot begin activity B or activity E (a critical path activity) until activity A is completed. Activity A has three days float and is not on the critical path. A team member, a vendor, and a nonteam member work overtime to complete activity A within its float time. You need to reimburse the nonteam member's department and pay the vendor at an overtime rate. What action should you take?

- A. Send a complaint letter to the key team member's boss, and ask him to fund the extra cost expended.
- B. Reevaluate your communications management plan.
- C. Thank the others for filling in, but tell them not to waste time on noncritical path activities.
- D. Pay the cost out of your project reserves.

*(Answer, p 147)*

## Question 129 of 200:

Your department is currently working on four urgent projects when it is assigned a major new project. To staff the new project, one of the four urgent projects needs to be terminated. The benefit cost ratios (BCR) for the four projects are listed. Which would you select for termination?

A. 0.8
B. 1.1
C. 0.9
D. 1.9

*(Answer, p 148)*

## Question 130 of 200:

Contract closure is similar to administrative closure in that they both involve:

A. product verification.
B. kickoff meetings.
C. quality assurance activities.
D. creation of the scope verification plan.

*(Answer, p 148)*

A project involves arranging for the closing of the company office where the team works and relocating everyone to a new city. The BEST thing the project manager can do is:

- A. spend time carefully creating the work breakdown structure.
- B. have a strong quality control plan.
- C. decrease the fringe benefits.
- D. carefully consider the reward system for the project.

*(Answer, p 148)*

**Question 132 of 200:**

Which of the following BEST describes what is included in a staffing management plan?

- A. A plan regarding what details about the project should go to whom and when the details need to be sent
- B. How the team will implement the plans for ensuring the project will satisfy the needs for which it was undertaken
- C. When and how human resources will be brought into and taken off the project team
- D. If independent estimates are needed, who will prepare them and when

*(Answer, p 149)*

## Question 133 of 200:

A project manager gets a call from a team member notifying him that there is a variance between the speed of a system on the project and the desired or planned speed. The project manager is surprised because that performance measurement was not identified in planning. If the project manager then evaluates whether the variance warrants a response, he is in what project management process?

- A. Initiating
- B. Executing
- C. Monitoring and controlling
- D. Closing

*(Answer, p 149)*

## Question 134 of 200:

After analyzing the status of your project, you determine that the earned value (EV) is lower than the planned value (PV). What should you expect as an outcome if this trend continues?

- A. The actual cost will be lower than planned.
- B. The estimate at completion will be lower than planned.
- C. The project will finish behind schedule.
- D. The project will finish below the original cost estimate.

*(Answer, p 149)*

A new project manager has been hired in your company, and you have been asked to mentor her. Because she is well trained, she is planning her project in great detail. Her first project for the company is relatively low priority, and you feel that the project manager is planning too many project control meetings. Which of the following would be the BEST thing to tell her?

- A. Strike a balance between the extent of the control system and the risk of unfavorable project outcomes.
- B. Make sure you identify more than 40 risks, and then have more than one meeting a month.
- C. A good project management plan should be about 90 percent complete before starting work.
- D. Make sure you include milestones to help plan the project to the project charter.

*(Answer, p 150)*

## Question 136 of 200:

Your company is concerned about improving its project performance. Internal measures have been created and have helped show areas needing improvement. Additional measures of performance are still needed. Which of the following would be the BEST thing to do?

A. Calculate the benefit to cost of purchasing a new piece of equipment.

B. Determine the project scope and measures to ensure the scope is met.

C. Perform a root cause analysis on the quality problems that have occurred on the project.

D. Read a project management magazine each month, and look at the results of other companies' projects to help determine quality measures for future projects.

*(Answer, p 150)*

You have just been assigned as project manager for a large telecommunications project. This one-year project is about halfway done. The project team consists of five sellers and 20 of your company's employees. You want to understand who is responsible for doing what on the project. Where would you find such information?

A. Responsibility assignment matrix
B. Resource histogram
C. Bar chart
D. Project organization chart

*(Answer, p 151)*

## Question 138 of 200:

A project has a tight budget when you begin negotiating with a seller for a piece of equipment. The seller has told you that the equipment price is fixed. Your manager has told you to negotiate the cost with the seller. What is your BEST course of action?

A. Make a good faith effort to find a way to decrease the cost.
B. Postpone negotiations until you can convince your manager to change her mind.
C. Hold the negotiations, but only negotiate other aspects of the project.
D. Cancel the negotiations.

*(Answer, p 151)*

## Question 139 of 200:

Two months into a design project, the customer requested a modification to the product. The change was made without notifying the project manager. During the final testing phase, results were different then what was planned for. This scenario is BEST thought of as an example of which of the following?

A. Poor scope control
B. Poor adherence to the communications management plan
C. Poor development of the quality management plan
D. Poor definition of the test plan

*(Answer, p 151)*

## Question 140 of 200:

Your company is in competition to win a major project for the government of a country. Your contacts in that country inform you that you must make a large payment to the foreign minister to be considered for the project. What should you do?

A. Inform your company's management, and ask for direction.
B. Do not make the payment.
C. Have the local contact make the payment.
D. Make the payment.

*(Answer, p 152)*

A team member notifies the project manager that a quality measurement for the project cannot be met. What is the LEAST effective thing for the project manager to do?

- A.   Notify management.
- B.   Hold a team meeting.
- C.   Look for alternative ways to meet the quality level.
- D.   Ask management to come up with options.

*(Answer, p 152)*

**Question 142 of 200:**

All of the following would occur during the closure of the project EXCEPT:

- A.   creating lessons learned.
- B.   formal acceptance.
- C.   reducing resource spending.
- D.   performing benefit cost analysis.

*(Answer, p 152)*

## Question 143 of 200:

Pareto charts help the project manager:

- A. focus on the most critical issues to improve quality.
- B. focus on stimulating thinking.
- C. explore a desired future outcome.
- D. determine if a process is out of control.

*(Answer, p 152)*

## Question 144 of 200:

While testing the strength of concrete poured on your project, you discover that over 35 percent of the concrete does not meet your company's quality standards. You feel certain the concrete will function as it is, and you don't think the concrete needs to meet the quality level specified. What should you do?

- A. Change the quality standards to meet the level achieved.
- B. List in your reports that the concrete simply "meets our quality needs."
- C. Ensure that the remaining concrete meets the standard.
- D. Report the lesser quality level and try to find a solution.

*(Answer, p 153)*

The communications management plan is developed
to meet the needs of the:

   A.    project sponsor.

   B.    team.

   C.    project manager.

   D.    stakeholders.

*(Answer, p 153)*

**Question 146 of 200:**

The customer responsible for overseeing your project
asks you to provide a written cost estimate that is
30 percent higher than your estimate of the project's
cost. He explains that the budgeting process requires
managers to estimate pessimistically to ensure enough
money is allocated for projects. What is the BEST way
to handle this?

   A.    Add the 30 percent as a lump sum contingency
fund to handle project risks.

   B.    Add the 30 percent to your cost estimate by
spreading it evenly across all project activities.

   C.    Create one cost baseline for budget allocation
and a second one for the actual project
management plan.

   D.    Ask for information on risks that would cause
your estimate to be too low.

*(Answer, p 153)*

The policies, methodologies, and templates for managing projects within the organization should be supplied by the:

  A.  project sponsor.
  B.  functional department.
  C.  project management office.
  D.  project manager.

*(Answer, p 154)*

A project manager discovers a defect in a deliverable due to the customer under contract today. The project manager knows the customer does not have the technical understanding to notice the defect. The deliverable meets the contract requirements, but it does not meet the project manager's quality standard. What should the project manager do in this situation?

  A.  Issue the deliverable, and get formal acceptance from the customer.
  B.  Note the problem in the lessons learned so future projects do not encounter the same problem.
  C.  Discuss the issue with the customer.
  D.  Inform the customer that the deliverable will be late.

*(Answer, p 154)*

## Question 149 of 200:

Many more changes were made to the project during the project executing processes than had been expected. What is the BEST thing for the project manager to do now?

- A. Wait until all changes are known, print out a new schedule, and revise the baseline.
- B. Make changes as needed, but maintain a schedule baseline.
- C. Make only the changes approved by management.
- D. Talk to management before any changes are made.

*(Answer, p 154)*

## Question 150 of 200:

A project manager has a problem with a team member's performance. What is the BEST form of communication for addressing this problem?

- A. Formal written communication
- B. Formal verbal communication
- C. Informal written communication
- D. Informal verbal communication

*(Answer, p 155)*

## Question 151 of 200:

You are managing a six-month project and have held biweekly meetings with your project stakeholders. After five-and-a-half months of work, the project is on schedule and budget, but the stakeholders are not satisfied with the deliverables. This situation will delay the project completion by one month. The MOST important process that could have prevented this situation is:

   A.   risk monitoring and control.
   B.   schedule control.
   C.   scope planning.
   D.   scope control.

*(Answer, p 155)*

## Question 152 of 200:

You are beginning a new project that has been attempted, but unsuccessful, several times in the past few years. Previous projects were cancelled because of "politics" (differing views and direction by key stakeholders on the project). This is an example of:

   A.   stakeholder analysis.
   B.   scope management.
   C.   historical information.
   D.   risk identification.

*(Answer, p 156)*

Scope decomposition involves subdividing the major project deliverables into smaller pieces to:

A. improve the accuracy of estimates, define a baseline for performance, and assist with responsibility assignments.
B. provide more activities to assign to resources.
C. provide the project duration, provide project control, and assign control charts.
D. assist in stakeholder assignment to project activities.

*(Answer, p 156)*

Which of the following BEST explains why the team needs to approve the final schedule?

A. To ensure activities can be completed as scheduled
B. To enhance team buy-in and loyalty
C. To get a better cost estimate
D. To improve communications

*(Answer, p 156)*

## Question 155 of 200:

What should be done with risks on the watchlist?

- A. Document them for historical use on other projects.
- B. Document them, and then revisit them during project monitoring and controlling.
- C. Document them, and set them aside because they are already covered in your contingency plans.
- D. Document them, and give them to the customer.

*(Answer, p 157)*

## Question 156 of 200:

Project A has had ineffective project meetings since its inception. There have been complaints that information does not get to the right people, some people are talking too much during the meeting, and the right people are not there to resolve issues. What is MOST likely missing from this project?

- A. A project scope management plan
- B. A staffing management plan
- C. A communications management plan
- D. A process improvement plan

*(Answer, p 157)*

## Question 157 of 200:

What is the LAST thing that occurs in project closure?

- A. Formal acceptance is received.
- B. Lessons learned are created.
- C. Financial closure is achieved.
- D. Resources are released.

*(Answer, p 157)*

## Question 158 of 200:

Which of the following is an output of the procurement management process?

- A. A contract
- B. Proposals
- C. Formal acceptance
- D. Change orders

*(Answer, p 158)*

## Question 159 of 200:

For which of the following actions could a project manager incur a fine and be jailed?

- A. Using people from outside the project manager's country to work on the project
- B. Failing to file the necessary permits in their own country
- C. Paying a bribe to a foreign official
- D. Not using minority workers on the project

*(Answer, p 158)*

## Question 160 of 200:

A project manager has just been assigned a team that comes from many countries, including Brazil, Japan, the U.S., and Britain. What is her BEST tool for success?

   A.   The responsibility assignment matrix (RAM)
   B.   The teleconference
   C.   Team communication with the WBS
   D.   Communication and well-developed people skills

*(Answer, p 158)*

## Question 161 of 200:

You are about to begin negotiations with people from another country. Which of the following should provide guidance on what business practices are allowed and not allowed?

   A.   The company code of conduct
   B.   The project charter
   C.   The project scope management plan
   D.   The negotiation plan

*(Answer, p 159)*

## Question 162 of 200:

A project manager has to resolve two problems. Both problems can occur in a single trial. In this situation, what is the BEST action the project manager can take?

A. Develop a solution for each problem.
B. Develop a solution that solves both problems.
C. Use a statistically independent trial.
D. No solution is needed, the two problems cancel each other out.

*(Answer, p 159)*

## Question 163 of 200:

A project manager is working on his first project with outside sellers. He is familiar with project control systems but not contract control systems. In explaining how a contract control system differs from a project control system, it is BEST to point out that a contract control system:

A. includes procedures.
B. includes trend analysis.
C. requires more sign-offs.
D. requires less documentation.

*(Answer, p 159)*

## Question 164 of 200:

During risk identification, a project manager identifies a risk that a fire could occur in the building during the testing, no matter what the company does. It would be BEST to _____ the risk.

   A.   deflect
   B.   accept
   C.   avoid
   D.   change

*(Answer, p 160)*

## Question 165 of 200:

Your project team is spending so much time reviewing potential changes to a project that you do not have time to complete project work. Which of the following is the LEAST likely reason for this problem?

   A.   No change control board
   B.   Not enough of an effort to identify the project stakeholders
   C.   A poor communications management plan
   D.   An unclear project charter

*(Answer, p 160)*

A seller has withdrawn from a project midway through the project executing processes, and another seller is taking over. The project manager meets with the replacement seller and his crew. In this meeting, what should the project manager do FIRST?

A.   Introduce the team members, and identify the roles and responsibilities.

B.   Communicate the objectives of the project.

C.   Review the schedule.

D.   Create a communications management plan.

*(Answer, p 160)*

**Question 167 of 200:**

From the project perspective, quality attributes:

A.   determine how effectively the performing organization supports the project.

B.   provide the basis for judging the project's success or failure.

C.   are specific characteristics for which a product is designed and tested.

D.   are objective criteria that must be met.

*(Answer, p 160)*

A project manger is in a meeting with the customer when the customer starts to yell about the fact that a change she requested will result in a delay to the project schedule. Interestingly, yelling is not a common practice in the client's culture. The project manager starts to explain why the change affected the schedule when the project manager's boss stops the meeting and carefully removes the project manager from the room. Which of the following would BEST describe what is going on?

- A. There was an inadequate change control system.
- B. The project manager did not inform the boss before the meeting.
- C. The project manager did not properly interpret the customer's communication.
- D. There was an inadequate agenda for the meeting.

*(Answer, p 161)*

## Question 169 of 200:

A project has faced major difficulties in the quality of its deliverables. Management now states that quality is the most important project constraint. If another problem with quality were to occur, what would be the BEST thing for the project manager to do?

- A. Fix the problem as soon as possible.
- B. Allow the schedule to slip by cutting cost.
- C. Allow cost to increase by fixing the root cause of the problem.
- D. Allow risk to increase by cutting cost.

*(Answer, p 162)*

## Question 170 of 200:

The sponsor wants the project to begin, but needs to be sure the appropriate amount of funding is available. The project manager wants to create the project estimate herself. Which of the following is the BEST rationale the project manager can use to convince the sponsor to allow her to prepare the project estimate?

- A. Such estimating provides a basis for monitoring and controlling.
- B. Such estimating gives the project manager an understanding of the sponsor's expectations.
- C. Such estimating will include hidden costs.
- D. A project estimate does not require the identification of work packages.

*(Answer, p 162)*

## Question 171 of 200:

Which of the following conflict resolution techniques will generate the MOST lasting solution?

A. Forcing
B. Smoothing
C. Compromise
D. Problem solving

*(Answer, p 163)*

## Question 172 of 200:

You have just been assigned as project manager for a large manufacturing project. This one-year project is about halfway done. It involves five different sellers and 20 members of your company on the project team. You want to quickly review where the project now stands. Which of the following reports would be the MOST helpful in finding such information?

A. Work status
B. Progress
C. Forecast
D. Communications

*(Answer, p 163)*

As a project manager, you are presented with the following information on the payback period for several possible projects. Which project is your BEST choice?

A.   Project A with a payback period of 6 months
B.   Project B with a payback period of 9 months
C.   Project C with a payback period of 12 months
D.   Project D with a payback period of 18 months

*(Answer, p 163)*

**Question 174 of 200:**

Which of the following techniques is the BEST way to determine project objectives?

A.   Delphi
B.   Earned value
C.   Expert interviews
D.   Pareto

*(Answer, p 163)*

## Question 175 of 200:

A project manager is putting his project control system in place. After a few meetings with others, he realizes that there are few effective measures of progress that can be used on the project. If you were to advise him, what would be the BEST thing the project manager can plan to do to control the project?

    A.    Emphasize the creation of milestones.

    B.    Add more people to the project team to help control it.

    C.    Have meetings every week versus every month.

    D.    Break the project into phases.

*(Answer, p 164)*

## Question 176 of 200:

A family member has a copy of a software program. He offers it to you at no cost because it will solve a business problem you have discussed with him. What should you do?

    A.    Do not accept the software, and advise the family member that such activity is in violation of copyright law.

    B.    Refuse the software, and notify the owner of the software.

    C.    Accept the software, and use it until you are able to buy the software yourself.

    D.    Accept the software with thanks, since the software creator will not find out.

*(Answer, p 164)*

## Question 177 of 200:

Which of the following does NOT assess the value a project brings to an organization?

- A. Benefit cost analysis
- B. Net present value
- C. Value analysis
- D. Needs assessment

*(Answer, p 164)*

## Question 178 of 200:

Your project sponsor is extremely happy with the project performance to date. To celebrate, he wants to hold a party with dancing and liquor for the entire team. You are concerned because the company policy states that "no alcohol can be served at company events." What should you do?

- A. The project sponsor is responsible. Hold the event as a good team-building experience.
- B. Inform human resources that the sponsor is serving alcohol at a company function.
- C. Tell the project sponsor that the party is a great idea, but no alcohol can be served.
- D. Suggest the event be held outside of working hours.

*(Answer, p 165)*

## Question 179 of 200:

Testing the entire population would:

- A. take too long.
- B. provide more information than wanted.
- C. be mutually exclusive.
- D. show many defects.

*(Answer, p 165)*

## Question 180 of 200:

A manufacturing project has a schedule performance index (SPI) of 0.89 and a cost performance index (CPI) of 0.91. Generally, what is the BEST explanation for why this occurred?

- A. The scope was changed.
- B. A supplier went out of business, and a new one needed to be found.
- C. Additional equipment needed to be purchased.
- D. A critical path activity took longer and needed more labor hours to complete.

*(Answer, p 165)*

## Question 181 of 200:

The project manager's role during the executing process group of the project can BEST be described as a(n):

    A.   director.

    B.   integrator.

    C.   coordinator.

    D.   leader.

*(Answer, p 166)*

## Question 182 of 200:

Which of the following regarding performance reporting is CORRECT?

    A.   It is done during project planning and project executing.

    B.   It is done during project planning and project monitoring and controlling.

    C.   It is done during project monitoring and controlling and project closure.

    D.   It is done during project executing and project monitoring and controlling.

*(Answer, p 166)*

## Question 183 of 200:

When is it BEST to perform administrative closure?

- A. At the end of project planning
- B. During project closure
- C. At the end of each project phase.
- D. At the beginning of the project with verification throughout the project

*(Answer, p 166)*

## Question 184 of 200:

You are a project manager for a small construction project. Your project was budgeted for U.S. $72,000 over a six-week period. As of today, you have spent U.S. $22,000. The earned value is U.S. $24,000. According to your schedule, you should have spent U.S. $30,000 by this time. Based on these circumstances, your project could be BEST described as:

- A. ahead of schedule.
- B. behind schedule.
- C. on schedule.
- D. having not enough information provided.

*(Answer, p 167)*

## Question 185 of 200:

Management has promised you part of the incentive fee from the customer if you complete the project early. While finalizing a major deliverable, your team informs you that the deliverable meets the requirements in the contract but will not provide the functionality the customer needs. If the deliverable is late, the project will not be completed early. What action should you take?

- A. Provide the deliverable as it is.
- B. Inform the customer of the situation, and work out a mutually agreeable solution.
- C. Start to compile a list of delays caused by the customer to prepare for negotiations.
- D. Cut other activities in a way that will be unnoticed to provide more time to fix the deliverable.

*(Answer, p 167)*

## Question 186 of 200:

The customer on a project tells the project manager he has run out of money to pay for the project. What should the project manager do FIRST?

- A. Shift more of the work to later in the schedule to allow time for the customer to get the funds.
- B. Enter administrative closure.
- C. Stop work.
- D. Release part of the project team.

*(Answer, p 167)*

## Question 187 of 200:

The contract statement of work is completed on a project. However, the customer is not happy because she wants additional work to be completed. In light of this, what should be done?

- A. Begin closure on the contract, and sign a new one for the additional work.
- B. Change to a cost reimbursable contract.
- C. Tell the customer it is too late to make a change.
- D. Add to the contract statement of work, and proceed with additional work after obtaining management's agreement.

*(Answer, p 168)*

## Question 188 of 200:

Which of the following is a common problem in administrative closure?

- A. Retaining resources to complete the project
- B. Completing the quality assurance plan
- C. Obtaining scope verification
- D. Completing a project charter

*(Answer, p 168)*

## Question 189 of 200:

An employee approaches you and asks to tell you something in confidence. He advises you that he has been performing illegal activities within the company for the last year. He is feeling guilty about it and is telling you in order to receive advice as to what he should do. What should you do?

A. Ask for full details.

B. Confirm that the activity is really illegal.

C. Inform your manager of the illegal activity.

D. Tell the employee to inform his boss.

*(Answer, p 168)*

## Question 190 of 200:

You are a new project manager for Company B. You previously worked for Company A, which had an extensive project management practice. Company B has its own procedures, but you are more familiar with those from Company A. You should:

A. use the practices from Company A but include any forms from Company B.

B. use the forms from Company B and begin to instruct them on ways to upgrade their own.

C. talk about changes to the change control board of Company B.

D. interact with others in an ethical way by sharing the good aspects of Company A's procedures.

*(Answer, p 168)*

Documentation on a contract should include all of the following EXCEPT?

    A.   Approvals

    B.   Inspection reports

    C.   Correspondence

    D.   Customer's meeting minutes

*(Answer, p 169)*

**Question 192 of 200:**

All of the following are parts of perform quality control EXCEPT?

    A.   Cost of quality

    B.   Inspection

    C.   Control charts

    D.   Flowcharting

*(Answer, p 169)*

You are assigned to a project that senior management has already decided to outsource. As a project manager, you need to work with the contracts department to select the vendor and then oversee the vendor through project completion. Company policy requires that a project of this size go through a formal bid process. A vice president in your company tells you that his friend owns one of the companies that might bid on the project and that the company would be an excellent choice as a vendor. This vice president has a reputation for making or breaking careers. What is generally the BEST course of action?

A. Follow the bid process, and show the vice president why the favored vendor is or is not the best choice.

B. Obtain written permission to bypass the formal bid process.

C. Let the evaluation team know that management has a favorite vendor.

D. Let the contracts department handle the situation.

*(Answer, p 169)*

## Question 194 of 200:

During which step of procurement management would you make the LEAST use of expert judgment?

- A. Plan purchases and acquisitions
- B. Select sellers
- C. Contract closure
- D. Plan contracting

*(Answer, p 170)*

## Question 195 of 200:

Checklists, fishbone diagrams, and Pareto charts are ALL examples of:

- A. quality planning tools.
- B. quality control tools.
- C. quality assurance tools.
- D. parts of a project management plan.

*(Answer, p 170)*

## Question 196 of 200:

The project manager has just received a change from the customer that does not affect the project schedule and is easy to complete. What should the project manager do FIRST?

- A. Make the change happen as soon as possible.
- B. Contact the project sponsor for permission.
- C. Go to the change control board.
- D. Evaluate the other components of the "triple constraint."

*(Answer, p 170)*

## Question 197 of 200:

A project is in progress, and the project manager is working with the quality assurance department to improve stakeholders' confidence that the project will satisfy the quality standards. Which of the following is an output of this process?

A.  Quality problems
B.  Quality metrics
C.  Recommended corrective action
D.  Quality audits

*(Answer, p 171)*

## Question 198 of 200:

Which motivational theory says that what motivates people is the work itself, including such things as responsibility, self-actualization, and professional growth?

A.  Maslow
B.  Deming
C.  McGregor
D.  Herzberg

*(Answer, p 171)*

## Question 199 of 200:

The project team is working on an important and complex project that requires a lot of coordination. Under these circumstances, the BEST strategy is to:

A.  have a war room.
B.  hire a contractor.
C.  hold more meetings to get the word out.
D.  gain extra assistance from management.

*(Answer, p 171)*

## Question 200 of 200:

Project management processes can be categorized into five groups. The process groups are linked by the results they produce. The outputs of one often become the input to another. What is the MOST appropriate sequence of the five project management process groups?

A.  Initiating, planning, monitoring and controlling, executing, closing
B.  Initiating, executing, monitoring and controlling, planning, closing
C.  Initiating, planning, executing, monitoring and controlling, closing
D.  Initiating, monitoring and controlling, planning, executing, closing

*(Answer, p 172)*

# Rita's
# Pocket PMP® Exam
## Answers and Explanations

Answer: D

Explanation: The key word here is "cross-disciplinary." Cross-disciplinary means that the project covers more than one department or technical area of expertise. In such a case, a matrix organization is needed with representatives from each department or discipline.

*(Source: PMP® Exam Prep, 30)*

Answer: C

Explanation: Many people would want to do nothing. However, any person who does not provide accurate and truthful information on their application to PMI violates PMI's Code of Professional Conduct, and PMI should be informed. You would not address this yourself (choice B). It is not your responsibility to do so.

*(Source: PMP® Exam Prep, 413)*

Answer: B

Explanation: Projects often need their own reward systems to affect performance. Project managers should create such a system for each project.

*(Source: PMP® Exam Prep, 276)*

**Question 4 of 200:** *(p 4)*

Answer: C

Explanation: Operations and maintenance usually occur after the project is completed.

*(Source: PMP® Exam Prep, 71)*

**Question 5 of 200:** *(p 4)*

Answer: C

Explanation: First, you need to document the reasons why the customer will not sign off acceptance. Once you understand the issues, you can work with the team to resolve them.

*(Source: PMP® Exam Prep, 70)*

**Question 6 of 200:** *(p 5)*

Answer: B

Explanation: Due to the lack of detailed scope, you should not select a fixed price contract (choice A). Because the buyer wants to be in full control, the time and material contract (choice B) is the best option.

*(Source: PMP® Exam Prep, 372)*

**Question 7 of 200:** *(p 5)*

Answer: B

Explanation: The question asks about identifying work. Only choice B relates to identifying work, as a work breakdown structure is used to define all of the work required to complete the project.

*(Source: PMP® Exam Prep, 128)*

**Question 8 of 200:** *(p 6)*

Answer: B

Explanation: These are reasons projects are initiated.

*(Source: PMBOK® Guide, 81)*

**Question 9 of 200:** *(p 6)*

Answer: A

Explanation: The project charter documents the project description and need of the client.

*(Source: PMP® Exam Prep, 89)*

**Question 10 of 200:** *(p 7)*

Answer: C

Explanation: Party B is only required to deliver what is defined in the contract.

*(Source: PMP® Exam Prep, 389)*

**Question 11 of 200:** *(p 8)*

Answer: D

Explanation: The sooner such discoveries are made known to other project managers, the better you can improve the capabilities of colleagues in your company. It is part of a project manager's professional and social responsibility to build such capabilities. The discoveries should also be documented in the status report (choice B), especially if that report has a wider distribution.

*(Source: PMP® Exam Prep, 416)*

**Question 12 of 200:** *(p 9)*

   Answer: A

   Explanation: Communications planning involves identifying communication requirements, including the identification of any communication preferences. In this situation, "you remind the sponsor" indicates that the information is being communicated according to the plan. However, the plan does not reflect the needs of this stakeholder.

*(Source: PMP® Exam Prep, 303)*

**Question 13 of 200:** *(p 10)*

   Answer: B

   Explanation: In a functional organization, the functional manager is the team member's boss and probably also the project manager's boss.

*(Source: PMP® Exam Prep, 30)*

**Question 14 of 200:** *(p 10)*

   Answer: A

   Explanation: Be careful on these questions. They try to divert your attention with talk about a quality project, etc. Focus on the question. You need a preliminary project scope statement first.

*(Source: PMP® Exam Prep, 92)*

**Question 15 of 200:** *(p 11)*

Answer: D

Explanation: Value analysis is a way of making sure the least expensive way is found to do the work.

*(Source: PMP® Exam Prep, 201)*


**Question 16 of 200:** *(p 11)*

Answer: C

Explanation: Remember, the definition of a project: temporary and unique. Operations and maintenance are considered on-going activities, not temporary. Therefore, such work is not considered a project or part of a project.

*(Source: PMP® Exam Prep, 71)*


**Question 17 of 200:** *(p 12)*

Answer: D

Explanation: In quality planning, you are defining quality for the project and determining how quality will be measured. Benchmarking looks at past projects for improvement ideas and sets guidelines from which to measure quality performance.

*(Source: PMP® Exam Prep, 243)*

**Question 18 of 200:** *(p 12)*

   Answer: B

   Explanation: The group is using organizational process assets to improve their project. Although the incident just occurred, it was on another project. They are in quality planning.

   *(Source: PMP® Exam Prep, 241)*


**Question 19 of 200:** *(p 13)*

   Answer: C

   Explanation: Nothing in this question says the other hotel is cheaper than the company's hotel chain. Did you read it that way? An employee does not have the option of whether to follow company policy. Nor generally can a manager override company policy (choice A). Only the owner of the policy can do that. A project manager must follow policy; therefore, it is best to use the company's hotel (choice C).

   *(Source: PMP® Exam Prep, 413)*


**Question 20 of 200:** *(p 13)*

   Answer: D

   Explanation: This can be a tough question unless you realize that the project is being done for the customer. Yes, it is hard to say no to our managers.

   *(Source: PMP® Exam Prep, 27)*

## Question 21 of 200: *(p 14)*

Answer: B

Explanation: Operations and maintenance activities are not part of projects. The work to collect data, meet with operations and maintenance to explain the project, and other such activities should be included in the project.

*(Source: PMP® Exam Prep, 71)*

## Question 22 of 200: *(p 14)*

Answer: D

Explanation: Though all the choices seem like good ideas, there is only one best. Usually these questions can be reworded to, "What do you do next?" Integrating (choice B) is a great idea, but not all projects have another project with which to integrate. The project manager cannot move on (choice C) until the project is actually completed. That means administrative closure must occur. The only choice that relates to administrative closure is choice D. Once administrative closure is done, then throw a party!

*(Source: PMP® Exam Prep, 107)*

**Question 23 of 200:** *(p 15)*

Answer: B

Explanation: The stakeholders determine the project requirements and decide whether the project was a success. Choices A, C, and D are all subsets of "stakeholders."

*(Source: PMP® Exam Prep, 25)*

**Question 24 of 200:** *(p 15)*

Answer: B

Explanation: You need to draw a network diagram for this question. This diagram has two paths: Start–1–2–3–End and Start–1–4–End. The original length of the first path is 10 and the second is 9, making the first path critical and the length of the critical path 10. If Activity 4 now takes 10 weeks instead of 8, the critical path would change to Start–1–4–End and be 11 weeks long.

*(Source: PMP® Exam Prep, 158-170)*

**Question 25 of 200:** *(p 16)*

Answer: B

Explanation: Problem solving is considered to be the best way to resolve conflicts.

*(Source: PMP® Exam Prep, 285)*

**Question 26 of 200:** *(p 16)*

Answer: A

Explanation: Contract documentation includes requested and approved contract changes. A contract change is required to put in place the new limits.

*(Source: PMP® Exam Prep, 393)*

**Question 27 of 200:** *(p 17)*

Answer: C

Explanation: Because a project done in a matrix organization involves people from across the organization, communications are more complex.

*(Source: PMP® Exam Prep, 28)*

**Question 28 of 200:** *(p 17)*

Answer: C

Explanation: Quality assurance, of which an audit is part, focuses on processes, procedures, and standards. Though ISO may be thought of as a standard, audits are not required, so choice A cannot be best. The seller cannot generally control or review the customer's process, so choice B cannot be best. Choice D is more representative of a cost audit than a quality audit and so cannot be the best choice.

*(Source: PMP® Exam Prep, 244)*

**Question 29 of 200:** *(p 18)*

Answer: D

Explanation: The critical path does not change if the scope is the same. A more aggressive deadline simply means the project is two weeks behind.

*(Source: PMP® Exam Prep, 159)*

**Question 30 of 200:** *(p 18)*

Answer: C

Explanation: Here the only skilled third party is an arbitrator.

*(Source: PMP® Exam Prep, 389)*

**Question 31 of 200:** *(p 19)*

Answer: B

Explanation: Did you forget that in a matrix organization, the functional manager controls the resources?

*(Source: PMP® Exam Prep, 270)*

**Question 32 of 200:** *(p 19)*

Answer: C

Explanation: A watchlist is made up of low priority risks that qualitative risk analysis has determined are too low priority or low impact to move further in the risk process.

*(Source: PMP® Exam Prep, 337)*

**Question 33 of 200:** *(p 20)*

    Answer: A

    **Explanation:** Activities A and F have float and are not on the critical path.

(Source: PMP® Exam Prep, 159)

**Question 34 of 200:** *(p 21)*

    Answer: A

    **Explanation:** Choice C would have been done the first time there was a problem, not now. Because this is a small piece of the project and you have a low confidence level, it would be best to remove the seller from the project.

(Source: PMP® Exam Prep, 382, 389)

**Question 35 of 200:** *(p 22)*

    Answer: A

    **Explanation:** Since you have signed a confidentiality agreement, the only allowable choice is A.

(Source: PMP® Exam Prep, 413)

**Question 36 of 200:** *(p 22)*

Answer: B

Explanation: Although the issue relates to scope, integrated change control procedures should be followed.

*(Source: PMP® Exam Prep, 95)*

**Question 37 of 200:** *(p 23)*

Answer: C

Explanation: The project manager is an integrator. This is a question about your role as an integrator and communicator.

*(Source: PMP® Exam Prep, 85)*

**Question 38 of 200:** *(p 23)*

Answer: D

Explanation: Both critical paths have durations of 16 weeks. Since 16 is the longest duration of paths, you have two critical paths.

*(Source: PMP® Exam Prep, 158-170)*

**Question 39 of 200:** *(p 24)*

Answer: D

Explanation: An award fee contract apportions a "bonus" to the seller based on performance.

*(Source: PMP® Exam Prep, 373)*

Answer: B

Explanation: Choice A cannot be best because cutting scope decreases profits on this type of contract. Choice C cannot be best, as CPFF contracts generally do not limit fee increases. Choice D cannot be best, as the fee in a CPFF contract is usually paid out on a continuous basis during the life of the project. One of the ways to change the profit in a cost plus fixed fee contract is to invoice for items not chargeable to the project (choice B).

*(Source: PMP® Exam Prep, 372)*

Answer: B

Explanation: Many of these choices could be done, but ask yourself, "What is the most effective thing to do?" The party may well generate lessons learned, and recording them (choice A) would certainly be a good idea, but the question asked what to do first. There is a more immediate issue—the manager. Choice C could also be useful, but it would require taking some of all the stakeholders' time when there is only one stakeholder—the manager—who definitely has an issue. Besides, a good project manager would be holding regular meetings with the stakeholders already. Choice D might be a good idea, as the manager apparently is not communicating with the project manager. However, this would not absolutely make sure the manager does communicate.

The manager is, in effect, saying that he is not getting the information he needs. His lack of needed information is causing him to suggest more meetings. Too many meetings are a problem on projects. The concept of information distribution (choice B) is to determine who needs what information and plan how to get it to them. A great project manager does not just add meetings, but solves the real problem in the best way. That might take the form of changing a report or sending existing reports to different people rather than adding meetings. For these reasons, choice B is best.

*(Source: PMP® Exam Prep, 309)*

## Question 42 of 200: *(p 26)*

Answer: D

Explanation: Risk response planning receives input of prioritized risk ratings.

*(Source: PMP® Exam Prep, 140)*

**Question 43 of 200:** *(p 26)*

Answer: A

Explanation: Ask yourself, "What is the root cause problem?" Your first action would be to find out whether working with family members is a common practice in that country (choice A), as there is nothing inherently illegal in this activity. Then you would review qualifications (choice B). Choices C and D may not be necessary after choices A and B are done.

*(Source: PMP® Exam Prep, 421)*

**Question 44 of 200:** *(p 27)*

Answer: D

Explanation: Funding limit reconciliation most likely will affect the project schedule, since work will need to be moved to when funds will be available.

*(Source: PMP® Exam Prep, 205)*

**Question 45 of 200:** *(p 27)*

Answer: C

Explanation: A contract statement of work may be revised and refined as it moves through procurement.

*(Source: PMP® Exam Prep, 379)*

## Question 46 of 200: *(p 28)*

Answer: B

**Explanation:** The WBS is hierarchical; therefore each lower level is made of all the parts of the upper level segment. The first level should be your project life cycle, not products (choice A). The WBS is not listed in chronological order (choice C) nor should functional areas (choice D) organize it.

*(Source: PMP® Exam Prep, 128)*


## Question 47 of 200: *(p 28)*

Answer: A

**Explanation:** A WBS does not show dates or responsibility assignments (choices B and C). Those are included on the bar chart and possibly in the communications management plan. The business need (choice D) is shown in the project charter. Never thought that a WBS could be shown to the customer? Made you think! Of course it could be used for that purpose.

*(Source: PMP® Exam Prep, 131)*

### Question 48 of 200: *(p 29)*

Answer: A

Explanation: Remember that for variances, negative is bad. In this situation, both the variances are negative. To answer the question, first look for which one of the four choices exhibits negative variances for both cost and schedule. Choice B exhibits negative variance for cost and positive variance for schedule. Choice C exhibits positive variance for cost and negative variance for schedule. Choice D exhibits positive variances for both. Only choice A exhibits both cost and schedule variances as negative.

*(Source: PMP® Exam Prep, 207)*

### Question 49 of 200: *(p 29)*

Answer: B

Explanation: Because cost increase has already occurred, it makes more sense to inform stakeholders of actual events.

*(Source: PMP® Exam Prep, 349)*

### Question 50 of 200: *(p 30)*

Answer: A

Explanation: Choices B, C, and D are inputs to scope verification.

*(Source: PMBOK® Guide, 105)*

**Question 51 of 200:** *(p 30)*

Answer: B

Explanation: The PERT calculation is [P + (4M) + O] / 6. So this result would be be [9 + (4 x 8) + 1] / 6 = [9 + 32 + 1] / 6 = 42 / 6 = 7. You have to memorize the formula.

*(Source: PMP® Exam Prep, 156)*

**Question 52 of 200:** *(p 31)*

Answer: D

Explanation: The best way to deal with this problem is to discover the root cause. Only choice D does that.

*(Source: PMP® Exam Prep, 103)*

**Question 53 of 200:** *(p 31)*

Answer: C

Explanation: Think of schedule development as all the work necessary to finalize the schedule. All the activities listed, other than choice C, are parts of other processes.

*(Source: PMP® Exam Prep, 143)*

**Question 54 of 200:** *(p 32)*

Answer: D

Explanation: This is an example of conflict and a choice of conflict resolution techniques. The project manager is withdrawing.

*(Source: PMP® Exam Prep, 285)*

**Question 55 of 200:** *(p 32)*

Answer: D

Explanation: This estimate has a wide range. It is done during project initiating, when very little is known about the project.

*(Source: PMP® Exam Prep, 204)*

**Question 56 of 200:** *(p 33)*

Answer: D

Explanation: You need to tailor the reports to meet the needs of all of your stakeholders and not just one. Find out what each needs, and address those needs. This should be outlined in the communications management plan.

*(Source: PMP® Exam Prep, 311)*

**Question 57 of 200:** *(p 33)*

Answer: C

Explanation: The project manager must ensure that the necessary skills are developed as part of the project.

*(Source: PMP® Exam Prep, 280)*

**Question 58 of 200:** *(p 33)*

Answer: C

Explanation: The rule of seven applies here. If you have seven data points in a row on the same side of the mean, statistically the mean has shifted, calling for action to correct the problem.

*(Source: PMP® Exam Prep, 250)*

**Question 59 of 200:** *(p 34)*

Answer: D

**Explanation:** The activity described has float because there is a difference between the early start and late start. An activity that has float is probably not on the critical path. There is no information presented about lag (choice B) or progress (choice C), so choice D is the best answer.

*(Source: PMP® Exam Prep, 465)*

**Question 60 of 200:** *(p 34)*

Answer: C

**Explanation:** A phase or project must be formally closed and accepted.

*(Source: PMP® Exam Prep, 71)*

**Question 61 of 200:** *(p 35)*

Answer: A

**Explanation:** Did you notice that many of the choices here misuse terms? A near-critical path is one close in length to the actual critical path. If it were to have less float, it would delay the project, so choice B is not best. A delay in an activity that is on the critical path (choice C) will generally delay the project. A mandatory dependency (choice D) is one that requires an activity to be done before or after another activity. An activity with free float can be rescheduled without impacting the rest of the project, making A the best choice.

*(Source: PMP® Exam Prep, 159)*

**Question 62 of 200:** *(p 36)*

Answer: C

Explanation: Notice the use of the word "detailed." Such a budget should be created during the planning process group.

*(Source: PMP® Exam Prep, 39)*

**Question 63 of 200:** *(p 36)*

Answer: B

Explanation: Discovering nonvalue activities is part of process analysis: implementing the process improvement plan. Many people choose a quality audit (choice C). However, a quality audit relates to determining whether we are using the right processes and whether those processes are effective, rather than improving processes.

*(Source: PMP® Exam Prep, 244)*

**Question 64 of 200:** *(p 37)*

Answer: D

Explanation: A project manager must always evaluate the situation before recommending a corrective action or a change.

*(Source: PMP® Exam Prep, 245)*

**Question 65 of 200:** *(p 37)*

Answer: C

Explanation: A work authorization system (choice A) helps tell the team when work should begin on work packages. A change control system (choice B) helps track, approve or reject, and control changes. A project management information system (PMIS—choice D) helps the project manager know how the project is going. Only a configuration management system (choice C) addresses controlling documents.

*(Source: PMP® Exam Prep, 95)*

## Question 66 of 200: *(p 38)*

Answer: B

Explanation: A user of the project's product is always a stakeholder, while the others may or may not be.

*(Source: PMP® Exam Prep, 25)*

## Question 67 of 200: *(p 38)*

Answer: A

Explanation: Although all choices could cause difficulty, only choice A makes estimating impossible.

*(Source: PMP® Exam Prep, 197)*

## Question 68 of 200: *(p 38)*

Answer: A

Explanation: Identifying root causes is part of risk identification.

*(Source: PMP® Exam Prep, 337)*

**Question 69 of 200:** *(p 39)*

   Answer: A

   Explanation: The higher the benefit cost ratio, the better.

*(Source: PMP® Exam Prep, 216)*


**Question 70 of 200:** *(p 39)*

   Answer: B

   Explanation: In a weak matrix, the functional manager has the power. There is no such thing as a functional matrix, and a tight matrix means co-location.

*(Source: PMP® Exam Prep, 28)*


**Question 71 of 200:** *(p 40)*

   Answer: C

   Explanation: The independent estimate is most concerned with cost and comparing cost estimates with in-house estimates or with outside assistance.

*(Source: PMP® Exam Prep, 387)*


**Question 72 of 200:** *(p 40)*

   Answer: B

   Explanation: The issue here is managing people. Only the staffing management plan helps manage people.

*(Source: PMP® Exam Prep, 276)*

**Question 73 of 200:** *(p 41)*

Answer: B

Explanation: The project life cycle does incorporate a methodology—for doing the work—so choice A cannot be best. It is the product life cycle that spawns many projects, so choice C cannot be best. Project management activities are described in the project management process, so choice D cannot be best. The project life cycle is different for each industry, so choice B is the best answer.

*(Source: PMP® Exam Prep, 31)*

**Question 74 of 200:** *(p 41)*

Answer: B

Explanation: Notice that there are multiple "right answers." However, removing the team member (choice A) is too drastic. By this time, you would have built a team through team building. Removing one person might drastically change team dynamics. Though choices C and D could be done, they involve taking action without knowing the reason there was a problem. Choices C and D may not solve the problem, and the same problem could resurface. Only choice B gets to the root cause.

*(Source: PMP® Exam Prep, 287)*

Answer: C

Explanation: The normal response to a force majeure is to give an extension of time (choice D), not to terminate. However, this force majeure seems to have had such an impact that the construction company cannot go on.

*(Source: PMP® Exam Prep, 394)*

**Question 76 of 200:** *(p 42)*

Answer: A

Explanation: The fact that such a discussion is occurring indicates a lack of clarity as to why the customer requested the 2,000-call capacity. Generally, a difference in objectives is resolved in favor of the customer. However, it is the project manager's responsibility to inform the customer of other options.

*(Source: PMP® Exam Prep, 26)*

**Question 77 of 200:** *(p 43)*

Answer: D

Explanation: The key to answering this question is to understand that this is a severe situation with many problems—so many problems that it is clear the contract is not serving either party. Meeting with the customer (choice A) has already been done. Choice B is not a long-term solution, and choice C (saving time) does not address the problem of unclear scope. This is why it is best to start all over (yes, this happens in the real world) rather than the other choices. When a contract no longer serves the needs it was intended to serve, it can be renegotiated if the appropriate parties agree to this. D is the best choice.

*(Source: PMP® Exam Prep, 383)*

## Question 78 of 200: *(p 44)*

Answer: C

Explanation: Don't forget that according to Herzberg's Theory, salary (choice A) is not a motivating agent. Linkage (choice C) is very important to make the reward valuable to both the receiver and those who did not receive it. This is more important than giving a choice of reward (choice B) or presenting the reward in public (choice D).

*(Source: PMP® Exam Prep, 277)*

## Question 79 of 200: *(p 44)*

Answer: D

Explanation: Here again is a question with more than one right answer. Would asking for something in writing be the best way to communicate here? In this particular situation, asking for the concern to be in writing might alienate the stakeholders. Therefore choice A cannot be best. The issue log (choice C) is where the issue should be listed, but the situation does not say if the project manager knows what the stakeholders' concerns are. Therefore, C cannot be the best choice. Why not B? Notice the use of the words "all stakeholders." Why bother other stakeholders with this problem when the project manager already knows there may be some concern of Stakeholder A and B to address, not all stakeholders. Choice B refers to making a presentation. Presentations are formal verbal. This problem would likely require informal verbal communication in order to discover the real problem. Choice D is therefore the best choice.

*(Source: PMP® Exam Prep, 312)*

## Question 80 of 200: *(p 45)*

Answer: D

Explanation: Configuration management involves making sure that everyone is working off the same documents.

*(Source: PMP® Exam Prep, 95)*

**Question 81 of 200:** *(p 45)*

   Answer: D

   Explanation: Ideally, there is a change control system in place that should be followed to make changes in the project.

   *(Source: PMP® Exam Prep, 103)*

**Question 82 of 200:** *(p 45)*

   Answer: C

   Explanation: McGregor devised the Theories of X and Y. These are easy questions so you have time for the harder ones.

   *(Source: PMP® Exam Prep, 287)*

**Question 83 of 200:** *(p 46)*

   Answer: A

   Explanation: Straight line depreciation uses the same amount each time period.

   *(Source: PMP® Exam Prep, 217)*

**Question 84 of 200:** *(p 46)*

   Answer: A

   Explanation: We assume that proper project management was followed and your opinion was considered during project initiating. Therefore, the best choice would be choice A. You need to provide the work as approved by management.

   *(Source: PMP® Exam Prep, 411)*

**Question 85 of 200:** *(p 47)*

Answer: A

Explanation: In a functional organization, the project manager has the least support for the project and has little authority to assign resources. Choices C and D are forms of weak matrix.

*(Source: PMP® Exam Prep, 30)*

**Question 86 of 200:** *(p 47)*

Answer: A

Explanation: Choice A represents reward power and is always one of the most effective choices, especially if there is room in the project budget. Choice B is penalty power and is the least effective choice. Although choice C is also reward power, the people who are receiving the reward are not in the position to assist with the specific problems listed in the question. Expert power (choice D) is generally a good choice, although in this case, the expertise is technical and the project manager may not be the technical expert on the project.

*(Source: PMP® Exam Prep, 282)*

### Question 87 of 200: *(p 48)*

Answer: C

Explanation: Notice the use of the terms "product" and "project scope" and how they mean different things? Choice C is the best option, since a change to any part of the product or project should be evaluated for impacts to other parts.

*(Source: PMP® Exam Prep, 123)*

### Question 88 of 200: *(p 48)*

Answer: D

Explanation: You need to consider the needs of all your stakeholders.

*(Source: PMP® Exam Prep, 26)*

### Question 89 of 200: *(p 49)*

Answer: A

Explanation: Choice B might help make sure things get done on time and that people know what work they need to do and when, but it is not related to quality. Choice C is looking backward. It is reactive, so it is not the best choice. Choice D deals with when people will be moved on and off the project. It does not deal with quality. Choice A is a better answer, because it directly deals with quality.

*(Source: PMP® Exam Prep, 244)*

## Question 90 of 200: *(p 49)*

Answer: D

Explanation: To ensure clear, concise communications, the project manager must manage communications by deciding what form of communication is best.

*(Source: PMP® Exam Prep, 305)*

## Question 91 of 200: *(p 50)*

Answer: C

Explanation: This is a professional and social responsibility/procurement/cost question. The situation described involves a claim. The best thing to do would be to get supporting information to find out what happened and take corrective action for the future. After choice C and negotiation, choice A would most likely occur. Choice D is unethical. Choice B is a meeting with YOUR management and should not occur until you have all the information.

*(Source: PMP® Exam Prep, 197)*

## Question 92 of 200: *(p 50)*

Answer: B

Explanation: You don't want to jump the gun and say that you are unable to meet the date (choice D) until after you have evaluated both crashing and fast tracking the project. Here the answer is to fast track, or do more activities in parallel (choice B).

*(Source: PMP® Exam Prep, 173)*

**Question 93 of 200:** *(p 51)*

   Answer: A

   Explanation: Your communication needs to be correct for the situation. Because situations vary, so must your communication methods.

   *(Source: PMP® Exam Prep, 305)*


**Question 94 of 200:** *(p 51)*

   Answer: B

   Explanation: A project manager must be more in control of the project than choices C and D reflect. Choice A is a common error many project managers make. Instead, the project manager should be controlling the project throughout the completion of the project.

   *(Source: PMP® Exam Prep, 181)*


**Question 95 of 200:** *(p 52)*

   Answer: C

   Explanation: A Pareto chart (choice A) might help the project manager decide which problems to focus on, but it does little to find the root cause of problems. Though the project is troubled, there is nothing to use conflict resolution techniques with (choice B), because the real problem has not been identified. Trend analysis (choice D) does not deal with root causes; it deals more with predicting the future. The best choice is C.

   *(Source: PMP® Exam Prep, 248)*

**Question 96 of 200:** *(p 52)*

Answer: B

Explanation: Nonverbal communication carries 55 percent of the message you send. With this much at stake, nonverbal communication is of major importance.

*(Source: PMP® Exam Prep, 304)*

**Question 97 of 200:** *(p 53)*

Answer: A

Explanation: Activity lists (choice B) may list the work package they relate to, but they do not contain detailed descriptions of the work packages. The preliminary project scope statement (choice C) may contain project scope, but it does not describe the work a team member is assigned. The project scope management plan (choice D) describes how scope will be planned, managed, and controlled. It does not include a description of each work package. The WBS dictionary defines each element in the WBS. Therefore, descriptions of the work packages are in the WBS dictionary.

*(Source: PMP® Exam Prep, 132)*

**Question 98 of 200:** *(p 53)*

Answer: C

Explanation: The key words here are "identifying the quality standards."

*(Source: PMP® Exam Prep, 241)*

**Question 99 of 200:** (p 54)

Answer: C

Explanation: The quantitative risk analysis process aims to analyze numerically the probability of each risk and its consequence on project objectives. These risks are then diminished, if possible, in risk response planning. Here the word "may" is critical to let you know that you are in quantitative risk analysis rather than risk response planning.

*(Source: PMP® Exam Prep, 337)*

**Question 100 of 200:** (p 54)

Answer: C

Explanation: Contacting the employee's manager and arranging a meeting is the best way to handle this discreetly and effectively. This does not consist of project-related activities, so resolution of the issue is not within the jurisdiction of the project manager.

*(Source: PMP® Exam Prep, 419)*

**Question 101 of 200:** (p 55)

Answer: B

Explanation: High-level stakeholders (choice A) are determined as part of the initiating process group. Choices C and D take place during the executing process group. Choice B is what goes on during a kickoff meeting, which is part of project planning.

*(Source: PMP® Exam Prep, 25)*

**Question 102 of 200:** *(p 55)*

    Answer: D

    Explanation: First you need to find out why the customer is not happy. Then meet with the team and determine options.

*(Source: PMP® Exam Prep, 103)*

**Question 103 of 200:** *(p 56)*

    Answer: D

    Explanation: Choice A refers to lessons learned, and choices B and C are always part of closure. When project closure occurs at the end of the project (as opposed to at the end of a phase), the project management plan would not need to be updated (choice D).

*(Source: PMP® Exam Prep, 70)*

**Question 104 of 200:** *(p 56)*

    Answer: B

    Explanation: Know the top four sources (schedules, project priorities, resources, and technical opinions) so you can answer questions such as this one. Don't be fooled because "personalities" is on the list. It is last.

*(Source: PMP® Exam Prep, 284)*

**Question 105 of 200:** *(p 56)*

Answer: B

Explanation: The formula is [N x (N − 1)] / 2. Therefore [9 x (8)] / 2 = 36. This question is really asking, "How many total communication channels are there?"

*(Source: PMP® Exam Prep, 307)*

**Question 106 of 200:** *(p 57)*

Answer: B

Explanation: Though all of these choices are correct things to do, the question asks what to do first. What is the most immediate problem? Isn't it most urgent to find out whether the concrete footings meet your project requirements? Choice A could be done, but it does not address the immediate concern. Choice C is excellent and is something many project managers might never think of doing. However, it does not address the immediate problem. Choice D is also not taking action to solve the problem. Are the concrete footings adequate? Only choice B will help you answer that.

*(Source: PMP® Exam Prep, 244)*

**Question 107 of 200:** *(p 57)*

Answer: A

Explanation: Nonverbal communication carries 55 percent of the message you send.

*(Source: PMP® Exam Prep, 304)*

**Question 108 of 200:** *(p 58)*

Answer: C

Explanation: Choice A is too passive for a project manager. Choice B means replacing the seller. It could be done but would probably result in a large time delay. Choice D is not ethical if it is done without the consent of the seller. This leaves only choice C.

*(Source: PMP® Exam Prep, 392)*

**Question 109 of 200:** *(p 58)*

Answer: D

Explanation: By definition, the most correct answer here is the project completion date.

*(Source: PMP® Exam Prep, 159)*

**Question 110 of 200:** *(p 59)*

Answer: C

Explanation: Recollections are less reliable than other documented results.

*(Source: PMP® Exam Prep, 90)*

**Question 111 of 200:** *(p 59)*

Answer: A

Explanation: Crashing is a cost/schedule trade-off. Since the project manager is not worried about her budget, but is worried about time, crashing is the most logical solution. Fast tracking (choice B) involves increased risk and so is not appropriate in this case.

*(Source: PMP® Exam Prep, 173)*

## Question 112 of 200: *(p 60)*

Answer: B

Explanation: Did the use of the word "resources" in the question cause you to select choice A? If so, you were tricked! The situation described is best thought of as what-if analysis.

*(Source: PMP® Exam Prep, 179)*

## Question 113 of 200: *(p 60)*

Answer: C

Explanation: There are many pieces of data in this question that are distracters from the real issue. Though it is common to have to cut costs (choice A) and add resources to a project (choice D), nothing in the question should lead you to think these will be required in this situation. Customers do not generally approve the project scope (what you are going to do to complete their requirements); instead, they approve the product scope (their requirements), so choice B cannot be best. Since the requirements are a measure of the completion of the product of the project (choice C), not having completed requirements makes such measurement impossible. This is why choice C is the best choice.

*(Source: PMP® Exam Prep, 126)*

## Question 114 of 200: *(p 61)*

Answer: B

Explanation: Reports help distribute information, not just report on progress.

*(Source: PMP® Exam Prep, 309)*

## Question 115 of 200: *(p 61)*

Answer: D

Explanation: The project management plan contains more than just a schedule, management plans, a budget (choice A), and the project manager's plan for managing and controlling, e.g. management plans (choice B). The project charter (choice C) is not part of the project management plan.

*(Source: PMP® Exam Prep, 94)*

## Question 116 of 200: *(p 61)*

Answer: B

Explanation: The key words here are "first two weeks." When you first organize a team, you need to provide the direction. After they become self-motivated, you could use one of the other leadership styles.

*(Source: PMP® Exam Prep, 283)*

## Question 117 of 200: *(p 62)*

Answer: A

Explanation: Know the difference between Theory X and Theory Y.

*(Source: PMP® Exam Prep, 288)*

## Question 118 of 200: *(p 62)*

Answer: B

Explanation: Product acceptance criteria is a part of the preliminary project scope statement.

*(Source: PMP® Exam Prep, 89)*

## Question 119 of 200: *(p 62)*

Answer: B

Explanation: The bar chart is the tool that shows the schedule at a detailed enough level for discussion with the team.

*(Source: PMP® Exam Prep, 180)*

## Question 120 of 200: *(p 63)*

Answer: A

Explanation: Having more resources does not generally make it HARDER to use reward power (choice B). Choice C is an incorrect statement. Choice D does not make sense, so it cannot be the correct answer. This leaves only choice A.

*(Source: PMP® Exam Prep, 307)*

## Question 121 of 200: *(p 63)*

Answer: B

Explanation: The rules of the Delphi Technique are: keep the experts' identities anonymous, do not bring the experts together in the same room, and build consensus.

*(Source: PMP® Exam Prep, 335)*

## Question 122 of 200: *(p 64)*

Answer: A

Explanation: Corrective action is anything done to bring expected future schedule performance in line with the project management plan. Such action should always be an output, but the other choices may not.

*(Source: PMP® Exam Prep, 182)*

## Question 123 of 200: *(p 64)*

Answer: C

Explanation: The risk response owner is assigned to carry out responses and must keep the project manager informed of any changes.

*(Source: PMP® Exam Prep, 344)*

## Question 124 of 200: *(p 65)*

Answer: B

Explanation: Compromising (choice A) is lose-lose, but it is not the worst choice. Smoothing (choice C) does not solve the problem. Do you wonder if forcing (choice B) is worse than withdrawal (choice D)? Withdrawal is a good thing to do when people need time to contemplate or get less annoyed. Forcing demands that others do what one person thinks should be done and, therefore, breeds animosity.

*(Source: PMP® Exam Prep, 285)*

**Question 125 of 200:** *(p 65)*

Answer: B

Explanation: All the choices listed, except choice B, are examples of transference or avoidance.

*(Source: PMP® Exam Prep, 342)*

**Question 126 of 200:** *(p 66)*

Answer: C

Explanation: Recommended corrective actions are outputs of scope verification and scope control.

*(Source: PMBOK® Guide, 113)*

**Question 127 of 200:** *(p 66)*

Answer: A

Explanation: The first choice would be to review the risk. Reserves may or may not be used, as in choice D.

*(Source: PMP® Exam Prep, 350)*

**Question 128 of 200:** *(p 67)*

Answer: B

Explanation: Notice that the issue of the key team member leaving has already occurred. Although the activity was not on the critical path, it would have impacted a critical path activity if it was not completed within its three-day float. Therefore, choice C is not correct. The best choice is to discover why the problem happened so you can prevent similar situations in the future. Only choice B looks at the cause of the problem.

*(Source: PMP® Exam Prep, 301)*

**Question 129 of 200:** *(p 68)*

  Answer: A

  Explanation: The lowest benefit cost ratio should be selected for termination.

*(Source: PMP® Exam Prep, 215)*


**Question 130 of 200:** *(p 68)*

  Answer: A

  Explanation: Kickoff meetings (choice B) occur during project planning. Quality assurance (choice C) occurs during project executing. A scope verification plan (choice D) is created earlier in the project and used during project monitoring and controlling, not closing. All types of closure must make sure the actual product of the project meets the requirements for the product. Therefore, choice A is the best answer.

*(Source: PMP® Exam Prep, 107, 395)*


**Question 131 of 200:** *(p 69)*

  Answer: D

  Explanation: Although choice A might help, it is not the best choice. Choice B really means, "spend the most time checking the work." Since it is after the fact and reactive, it is not the best choice for this situation. Choice C would only make things worse. Choice D is the correct answer.

*(Source: PMP® Exam Prep, 276)*

**Question 132 of 200:** *(p 69)*

    Answer: C

    Explanation: Choice A is a communications management plan. Choice B is a quality management plan. Choice D is part of a procurement management plan.

*(Source: PMP® Exam Prep, 276)*


**Question 133 of 200:** *(p 70)*

    Answer: C

    Explanation: Even though the measurement was not identified in planning, the project manager would still have to investigate the variance and determine if it is important. Therefore, the project manager is in the project monitoring and controlling process group.

*(Source: PMP® Exam Prep, 39)*


**Question 134 of 200:** *(p 70)*

    Answer: C

    Explanation: If EV is lower than PV, it indicates less work is occurring than was scheduled, resulting in schedule slippage.

*(Source: PMP® Exam Prep, 207)*

**Question 135 of 200:** *(p 71)*

Answer: A

Explanation: The number of risks identified (choice B) is dependent on the project, so choice B cannot be the best. There is a belief that a project management plan should be complete before starting work (choice C), but there are no standards that say it should be 90 percent complete or any other such number. That would also depend on the project. Milestones (choice D) might be a helpful control tool, but they are not used to "help plan the project to the project charter." This statement makes no sense. Since the project is lower priority, it would be wise to limit control activities to the needs of the project, making choice A the best choice.

*(Source: PMP® Exam Prep, 97)*

**Question 136 of 200:** *(p 72)*

Answer: D

Explanation: The question states that internal measures have already been created. Therefore, external ones are needed. Only choice D helps benchmark externally.

*(Source: PMP® Exam Prep, 243)*

**Question 137 of 200:** *(p 73)*

Answer: A

Explanation: The responsibility assignment matrix maps who will do the work. The resource histogram (choice B) shows the number of resources used in each time period. In its pure form, a bar chart (choice C) shows only activity and calendar date. An organizational chart (choice D) shows who reports to whom.

*(Source: PMP® Exam Prep, 275)*

**Question 138 of 200:** *(p 73)*

Answer: A

Explanation: There is always a way to decrease costs on the project. How about offering to feature the seller in your next television ad? The best choice is A.

*(Source: PMP® Exam Prep, 387)*

**Question 139 of 200:** *(p 74)*

Answer: A

Explanation: If the scope change had been properly recorded, the change impact could have been addressed immediately.

*(Source: PMP® Exam Prep, 135)*

**Question 140 of 200:** *(p 74)*

Answer: B

Explanation: Payments for nonroutine government actions are bribes and should not be paid.

*(Source: PMP® Exam Prep, 414)*

**Question 141 of 200:** *(p 75)*

Answer: A

Explanation: It is the project manager's job to take action to address this situation. Therefore, choice A is the least effective option. The other choices could help the project manager discover the reason for the problem.

*(Source: PMP® Exam Prep, 245)*

**Question 142 of 200:** *(p 75)*

Answer: D

Explanation: Benefit cost analysis (choice D) is done earlier in the project to help select between alternatives. All the other choices are done during closing. Therefore, choice D must be the best answer.

*(Source: PMP® Exam Prep, 106)*

**Question 143 of 200:** *(p 76)*

Answer: A

Explanation: Choices B and C relate to fishbone diagrams. Choice D relates to control charts. Only choice A relates to Pareto charts.

*(Source: PMP® Exam Prep, 249)*

## Question 144 of 200: *(p 76)*

Answer: D

Explanation: Can you explain why choices A and B are unethical? Choice C simply withdraws from the problem and is therefore not the best solution. The only possible choice is D. That choice would involve quality and other experts to find a resolution.

*(Source: PMP® Exam Prep, 413)*

## Question 145 of 200: *(p 77)*

Answer: D

Explanation: Choice D includes all of the other choices. Stakeholders can be project assets who perform project work, provide expert advice, and remove roadblocks. Because they are involved in the project, you should consider their needs when creating a communications management plan.

*(Source: PMP® Exam Prep, 308)*

## Question 146 of 200: *(p 77)*

Answer: D

Explanation: Presenting anything besides your original estimate to allocate more to the budget is inaccurate and calls into question your competence and integrity as a project manager. The customer should list potential changes and risks to your estimate. If the costs and risks are justified, you can increase the budget.

*(Source: PMP® Exam Prep, 199)*

**Question 147 of 200:** *(p 78)*

Answer: C

Explanation: This is the role of the project management office.

*(Source: PMP® Exam Prep, 23)*


**Question 148 of 200:** *(p 78)*

Answer: C

Explanation: Choice A does not follow the rule to protect the best interests of the customer. Choice B does not solve the problem. Choice D will cause a default of contract. Although the deliverable meets the contractual requirements, it is best to bring the problem to the customer's attention (choice C) so an option that does no harm can be found.

*(Source: PMP® Exam Prep, 413)*


**Question 149 of 200:** *(p 79)*

Answer: B

Explanation: The schedule baseline is there for you to determine how the project is progressing. Follow your change management process, and continue to track against your baseline.

*(Source: PMP® Exam Prep, 95)*

**Question 150 of 200:** *(p 79)*

Answer: D

Explanation: The best choice is D. If informal verbal communication does not solve the problem, choice A is the next best choice. This does not mean that you do not keep records of the problem, but this question is asking about communication between two parties.

*(Source: PMP® Exam Prep, 305)*

**Question 151 of 200:** *(p 80)*

Answer: C

Explanation: Choices A, B, and D are processes in the monitoring and controlling process group. This situation asks how to prevent the problem. This would have been done during the planning processes (choice C), as the project deliverables are defined in scope planning. Good planning reduces the likelihood of a similar situation by including the right people and spending adequate time in clarifying the project scope.

*(Source: PMP® Exam Prep, 125)*

**Question 152 of 200:** *(p 80)*

Answer: C

Explanation: This question shows how important historical information is for adequately planning projects. Notice the wording in the question. It is looking for an example. The word "stakeholder" is used in the question, but this is not an example of stakeholder analysis (choice A), nor is it an example of scope management (choice B) as the situation described is from past projects. Such information can lead to risks (choice D), but this is not an example of risk identification.

*(Source: PMP® Exam Prep, 90)*

**Question 153 of 200:** *(p 81)*

Answer: A

Explanation: Smaller pieces allow for more accurate estimates, are used to track the project against actuals, and are used to assign resources using a resource assignment matrix. Therefore, choice A is the best answer.

*(Source: PMP® Exam Prep, 128)*

**Question 154 of 200:** *(p 81)*

Answer: A

Explanation: The estimates received in the project management process before the final schedule are based on "how much or how long will it take." It is also important to check "when," on a calendar basis, the work can be done.

*(Source: PMP® Exam Prep, 155)*

**Question 155 of 200:** *(p 82)*

Answer: B

Explanation: Risks change throughout the project. You need to review risks at intervals during the project to ensure that noncritical risks have not become critical.

*(Source: PMP® Exam Prep, 337)*

**Question 156 of 200:** *(p 82)*

Answer: C

Explanation: The communications management plan helps people understand what needs to be communicated, to whom, when, and by what methods.

*(Source: PMP® Exam Prep, 308)*

**Question 157 of 200:** *(p 83)*

Answer: D

Explanation: Outputs of administrative closure include archives, lessons learned, and project closure. However, some project resources (people, computers, telephones) must be used to perform these activities. Once completed, the project can release its resources. Therefore choice D is best.

*(Source: PMP® Exam Prep, 72)*

**Question 158 of 200:** *(p 83)*

Answer: C

Explanation: This question is asking for the output of the procurement process as a whole, not an output of the pieces within the process. The procurement process should lead toward formal acceptance of the product of the project, making choice C the best choice. Be careful to properly read questions on the exam!

*(Source: PMP® Exam Prep, 396)*

**Question 159 of 200:** *(p 83)*

Answer: C

Explanation: Although some of the other choices might result in a fine, bribes can result in jail time.

*(Source: PMP® Exam Prep, 414)*

**Question 160 of 200:** *(p 84)*

Answer: D

Explanation: People from different cultures with different cultural values and beliefs stress the importance of understanding both the basic definitions and the areas of cultural impact. As project managers, we need to have good communication skills and a willingness to adapt to other cultures.

*(Source: PMP® Exam Prep, 308)*

**Question 161 of 200:** *(p 84)*

    Answer: A

    Explanation: The company code of conduct should cover items such as bribes, guidelines for situations, and other business practices.

        *(Source: PMP® Exam Prep, 414)*

**Question 162 of 200:** *(p 85)*

    Answer: A

    Explanation: The question indicates the two problems are unrelated. Therefore, they require separate solutions.

        *(Source: PMP® Exam Prep, 246)*

**Question 163 of 200:** *(p 85)*

    Answer: C

    Explanation: Both systems include procedures, so choice A is not correct. A contract control system requires more, not less, documentation, so choice D is not correct. A trend analysis (choice B) is not usually part of either system. This leaves only choice C. Contracts are legal documents and, therefore, generally require more sign-offs.

        *(Source: PMP® Exam Prep, 393)*

**Question 164 of 200:** *(p 86)*

Answer: A

Explanation: Remember that the word *avoid* (choice C) does not mean "prevent from happening." Rather, it means "eliminate the cause." Such risks are normally handled by purchasing insurance. *Deflect* is another word for *transfer*.

*(Source: PMP® Exam Prep, 164)*

**Question 165 of 200:** *(p 86)*

Answer: C

Explanation: A poor communications management plan is not likely to cause the volume of changes in this instance.

*(Source: PMP® Exam Prep, 362)*

**Question 166 of 200:** *(p 87)*

Answer: A

Explanation: It is important that the new seller understand who is who on the project (choice A). Choices B and C would be parts of the contract. Choice D might occur after choice A, but it is not first.

*(Source: PMP® Exam Prep, 267)*

**Question 167 of 200:** *(p 87)*

Answer: A

Explanation: Quality attributes are the measurements that determine if the product is acceptable. They are based on the characteristics of the product for which they were designed.

*(Source: PMP® Exam Prep, 249)*

## Question 168 of 200: *(p 88)*

Answer: C

Explanation: This question has many distracters. Choice D could not be best, because there is no indication that the agenda was inadequate. The situation does not indicate that the boss was not aware of the situation (choice B). He could have been aware of the problem of schedule delay and still, based on the situation, done the same thing. Why? The project manager did not correctly interpret the magnitude of the customer's anger and did not correctly receive the communication. The problem was that the customer was angry, and it was a bad communication choice to try to explain why the schedule was delayed. It might be best to withdraw. The customer was not ready to listen. After withdrawal, it would be best to review the change control system, because it is obvious something was missed in communicating changes and their effect on the customer.

*(Source: PMP® Exam Prep, 312)*

**Question 169 of 200:** *(p 89)*

Answer: C

Explanation: Many people would pick choice A. It is proactive, but choice C mentions root cause and the probable effect of dealing with the problem. If a problem with quality occurs again, some other project constraint(s) must change to accommodate fixing the problem. Choice B is partially correct (allow schedule to slip) but may not need to occur, because the project manager might be able to compress the schedule in other areas. Besides, cutting cost does not necessarily cause the schedule to slip. Choice D is not best, because a quality problem is most likely to create additional cost, rather than cut cost.

*(Source: PMP® Exam Prep, 245)*

**Question 170 of 200:** *(p 89)*

Answer: A

Explanation: Choice B generally comes from the sponsor's work. Choice C is a rationale for the project manager NOT to prepare the estimate. Choice D is an incorrect statement.

*(Source: PMP® Exam Prep, 204)*

### Question 171 of 200: *(p 90)*

Answer: D

Explanation: Problem solving normally takes more time, but it gets buy-in from everyone, generating a more lasting solution.

*(Source: PMP® Exam Prep, 285)*

### Question 172 of 200: *(p 90)*

Answer: B

Explanation: The key word is "quickly." The status report (choice A) is too detailed for a quick look. The forecast report (choice C) only looks into the future. The progress report (choice B) will summarize project status.

*(Source: PMP® Exam Prep, 311)*

### Question 173 of 200: *(p 91)*

Answer: A

Explanation: Pick the lower number.

*(Source: PMP® Exam Prep, 214)*

### Question 174 of 200: *(p 91)*

Answer: A

Explanation: Earned value (choice B) is a progress reporting tool. Pareto (choice D) is a quality tool. Expert interviews (choice C) simply provide information from individuals, while the Delphi technique (choice A) leads to consensus of expert opinion and is therefore best.

*(Source: PMP® Exam Prep, 87, 261)*

**Question 175 of 200:** *(p 92)*

Answer: A

Explanation: Adding more people (choice B) would increase cost. Since there is a less costly solution, this would not be the best choice. Many project managers make the mistake of just adding meetings (choice C), but there is usually a more effective and less costly use of time. Though phases (choices D) would help, these are usually larger pieces than milestones. Did you know that adding milestones (choice A) is a control feature? If a milestone is completed on time and on budget, the project manager has some measure of the status of the project.

*(Source: PMP® Exam Prep, 149)*

**Question 176 of 200:** *(p 92)*

Answer: A

Explanation: Do not violate copyright laws.

*(Source: PMP® Exam Prep, 413)*

**Question 177 of 200:** *(p 93)*

Answer: C

Explanation: Value analysis is a way of finding the least expensive way to do the work.

*(Source: PMP® Exam Prep, 201, 213)*

**Question 178 of 200:** *(p 93)*

Answer: C

Explanation: As the project manager, it is your professional and social responsibility to ensure that company policies are followed throughout the project.

*(Source: PMP® Exam Prep, 414)*


**Question 179 of 200:** *(p 94)*

Answer: A

Explanation: The length of time it takes to test a whole population is one of the reasons to take a sample.

*(Source: PMP® Exam Prep, 245)*


**Question 180 of 200:** *(p 94)*

Answer: D

Explanation: To answer this question, you must look for a choice that would take longer and cost more. If you picked choice A, reread it. It says scope was changed, not necessarily added to. If the change was to reduce the scope, it might also have reduced cost. Though it would take time to handle the event described in choice B, the impacted activity might not be on the critical path and thus might not affect time. Choice C would definitely add cost but not necessarily time. Only choice D would negatively affect both time and cost.

*(Source: PMP® Exam Prep, 207)*

# Question 181 of 200: *(p 95)*

Answer: B

Explanation: Directing (choice A) occurs while the project management plan is being created. During project executing, the project manager should be focused on integrating the work of others into a cohesive whole. This is more important than just coordinating (choice C) or leading (choice D).

*(Source: PMP® Exam Prep, 61)*


# Question 182 of 200: *(p 95)*

Answer: C

Explanation: Performance reporting is a control feature and is also done during closure to report the final performance of the project.

*(Source: PMP® Exam Prep, 311)*


# Question 183 of 200: *(p 96)*

Answer: C

Explanation: You want to capture data at the end of each phase of a project. If you wait until the end, you may forget important information.

*(Source: PMP® Exam Prep, 107)*

**Question 184 of 200:** *(p 96)*

Answer: B

**Explanation:** SPI = EV / PV. In this case SPI = 24,000 / 30,000, or 0.8. An SPI of 0.8 indicates that you are behind schedule.

*(Source: PMP® Exam Prep, 207)*

**Question 185 of 200:** *(p 97)*

Answer: B

**Explanation:** Choices A and D ignore the customer's best interests. Any delays would have already been resolved with other change orders, so choice C is not appropriate. The ethical solution is to talk with the customer (choice B). You might still be able to win the incentive fee and find a mutually agreeable solution. Think of the good will that will come from telling the customer.

*(Source: PMP® Exam Prep, 414)*

**Question 186 of 200:** *(p 97)*

Answer: B

**Explanation:** Every project must be closed, as administrative closure provides benefit to the performing organization. This makes stopping work (choice C) not the best choice. Choices A and D do not solve the problem—they just postpone dealing with it.

*(Source: PMP® Exam Prep, 395)*

### Question 187 of 200: *(p 98)*

Answer: A

Explanation: The customer signed for the work specified in the contract. If that work is complete, they may not add scope unless the formal change management process approves the change. At this late date, it would be better to complete this contract and begin a new one.

*(Source: PMP® Exam Prep, 395)*

### Question 188 of 200: *(p 98)*

Answer: A

Explanation: The biggest problem is retaining team members until closure of the project. People start looking for their next project and leave before administrative closure is complete.

*(Source: PMP® Exam Prep, 30)*

### Question 189 of 200: *(p 99)*

Answer: C

Explanation: You must report the activities.

*(Source: PMP® Exam Prep, 413)*

### Question 190 of 200: *(p 99)*

Answer: B

Explanation: You need to follow Company B's procedures while you try to influence improvement via the change management processes.

*(Source: PMP® Exam Prep, 414)*

**Question 191 of 200:** *(p 100)*

Answer: D

Explanation: A customer's meeting minutes have no impact on disputes that arise; therefore, they are not required.

*(Source: PMP® Exam Prep, 393)*

**Question 192 of 200:** *(p 100)*

Answer: A

Explanation: Tools and techniques for perform quality control include flowcharting, statistical sampling, Pareto charts, control charts, and inspection.

*(Source: PMBOK® Guide, 182)*

**Question 193 of 200:** *(p 101)*

Answer: A

Explanation: As a project manager, it is your responsibility to provide criteria to the contracts department based on the project needs and to protect your project along the way. Choice B is not practical. Choice C will increase the chance of incorrect results during the evaluation. Choice D is not correct project management practice.

*(Source: PMP® Exam Prep, 385)*

**Question 194 of 200:** *(p 102)*

Answer: C

Explanation: You need experts to assist in creating the terms and conditions of the contract and other experts to finalize the contract statement of work. These activities are done during plan contracting.

*(Source: PMBOK® Guide, 272)*


**Question 195 of 200:** *(p 102)*

Answer: B

Explanation: Although some of these tools can be used in quality planning, taken as a whole, they are ALL used only in perform quality control.

*(Source: PMP® Exam Prep, 247)*


**Question 196 of 200:** *(p 102)*

Answer: D

Explanation: The other impacts to the project should be evaluated first. Such impacts include cost, quality, scope, risk, and customer satisfaction. Once these are evaluated, the change control board, if one exists, can approve or deny the change.

*(Source: PMP® Exam Prep, 103)*

**Question 197 of 200:** *(p 103)*

Answer: C

Explanation: In this question, we are in quality assurance. An output of perform quality assurance is recommended corrective action (choice C). Since the purpose of quality management is to improve quality, quality problems (choice A) could not be an output of any of the quality processes. Choice B is an input to perform quality assurance. Choice D occurs during perform quality assurance—it is not an output of it.

*(Source: PMP® Exam Prep, 245)*


**Question 198 of 200:** *(p 103)*

Answer: D

Explanation: This is the essence of Herzberg's hygiene factors.

*(Source: PMP® Exam Prep, 288)*


**Question 199 of 200:** *(p 104)*

Answer: A

Explanation: Due to the high need for coordination, it is best to centralize the project management and control processes.

*(Source: PMP® Exam Prep, 280)*

**Question 200 of 200:** *(p 104)*

Answer: C

**Explanation:** Sometimes questions on the exam can be quite easy. This one tests whether you know how to organize the project management processes.

*(Source: PMP® Exam Prep, 37)*

# Rita's
# Pocket PMP® Exam
## Questions by Process Group

# Initiating

|  | Page |
|---|---|
| Question 1 . . . . . . . . . . . . . . . . . . . . . . . . | 2 |
| Question 8 . . . . . . . . . . . . . . . . . . . . . . . . | 6 |
| Question 9 . . . . . . . . . . . . . . . . . . . . . . . . | 6 |
| Question 13 . . . . . . . . . . . . . . . . . . . . . . . | 10 |
| Question 16 . . . . . . . . . . . . . . . . . . . . . . . | 11 |
| Question 20 . . . . . . . . . . . . . . . . . . . . . . . | 13 |
| Question 21 . . . . . . . . . . . . . . . . . . . . . . . | 14 |
| Question 23 . . . . . . . . . . . . . . . . . . . . . . . | 15 |
| Question 27 . . . . . . . . . . . . . . . . . . . . . . . | 17 |
| Question 66 . . . . . . . . . . . . . . . . . . . . . . . | 38 |
| Question 69 . . . . . . . . . . . . . . . . . . . . . . . | 39 |
| Question 73 . . . . . . . . . . . . . . . . . . . . . . . | 41 |
| Question 76 . . . . . . . . . . . . . . . . . . . . . . . | 42 |
| Question 85 . . . . . . . . . . . . . . . . . . . . . . . | 47 |
| Question 88 . . . . . . . . . . . . . . . . . . . . . . . | 48 |
| Question 118 . . . . . . . . . . . . . . . . . . . . . . | 62 |
| Question 147 . . . . . . . . . . . . . . . . . . . . . . | 78 |
| Question 152 . . . . . . . . . . . . . . . . . . . . . . | 80 |
| Question 173 . . . . . . . . . . . . . . . . . . . . . . | 91 |
| Question 174 . . . . . . . . . . . . . . . . . . . . . . | 91 |
| Question 177 . . . . . . . . . . . . . . . . . . . . . . | 93 |
| Question 200 . . . . . . . . . . . . . . . . . . . . . . | 104 |

## Planning

| | Page |
|---|---|
| Question 6. | 5 |
| Question 7. | 5 |
| Question 14. | 10 |
| Question 15. | 11 |
| Question 17. | 12 |
| Question 18. | 12 |
| Question 24. | 15 |
| Question 29. | 18 |
| Question 31. | 19 |
| Question 32. | 19 |
| Question 33. | 20 |
| Question 38. | 23 |
| Question 39. | 24 |
| Question 42. | 26 |
| Question 44. | 27 |
| Question 45. | 27 |
| Question 46. | 28 |
| Question 51. | 30 |
| Question 53. | 31 |
| Question 55. | 32 |
| Question 57. | 33 |
| Question 59. | 34 |
| Question 62. | 36 |
| Question 65. | 37 |
| Question 67. | 38 |

Question 68. . . . . . . . . . . . . . . . . . .*38*
Question 72. . . . . . . . . . . . . . . . . . .*40*
Question 78. . . . . . . . . . . . . . . . . . .*44*
Question 83. . . . . . . . . . . . . . . . . . .*46*
Question 90. . . . . . . . . . . . . . . . . . .*49*
Question 98. . . . . . . . . . . . . . . . . . .*53*
Question 99. . . . . . . . . . . . . . . . . . .*54*
Question 101. . . . . . . . . . . . . . . . . .*55*
Question 109. . . . . . . . . . . . . . . . . .*58*
Question 115. . . . . . . . . . . . . . . . . .*61*
Question 116. . . . . . . . . . . . . . . . . .*61*
Question 125. . . . . . . . . . . . . . . . . .*65*
Question 131. . . . . . . . . . . . . . . . . .*69*
Question 132. . . . . . . . . . . . . . . . . .*69*
Question 137. . . . . . . . . . . . . . . . . .*73*
Question 145. . . . . . . . . . . . . . . . . .*77*
Question 153. . . . . . . . . . . . . . . . . .*81*
Question 154. . . . . . . . . . . . . . . . . .*81*
Question 164. . . . . . . . . . . . . . . . . .*86*
Question 170. . . . . . . . . . . . . . . . . .*89*
Question 194. . . . . . . . . . . . . . . . . .*102*

# Executing

| | Page |
|---|---|
| Question 3 | 3 |
| Question 10 | 7 |
| Question 12 | 9 |
| Question 25 | 16 |
| Question 28 | 17 |
| Question 34 | 21 |
| Question 37 | 23 |
| Question 40 | 24 |
| Question 41 | 25 |
| Question 47 | 28 |
| Question 54 | 32 |
| Question 63 | 36 |
| Question 70 | 39 |
| Question 71 | 40 |
| Question 74 | 41 |
| Question 77 | 43 |
| Question 79 | 44 |
| Question 80 | 45 |
| Question 82 | 45 |
| Question 86 | 47 |
| Question 89 | 49 |
| Question 91 | 50 |
| Question 93 | 51 |
| Question 94 | 51 |
| Question 96 | 52 |
| Question 97 | 53 |

Question 102. . . . . . . . . . . . . . . . . . *55*
Question 104. . . . . . . . . . . . . . . . . . *56*
Question 105. . . . . . . . . . . . . . . . . . *56*
Question 106. . . . . . . . . . . . . . . . . . *57*
Question 107. . . . . . . . . . . . . . . . . . *57*
Question 108. . . . . . . . . . . . . . . . . . *58*
Question 110. . . . . . . . . . . . . . . . . . *59*
Question 114. . . . . . . . . . . . . . . . . . *61*
Question 117. . . . . . . . . . . . . . . . . . *62*
Question 119. . . . . . . . . . . . . . . . . . *62*
Question 120. . . . . . . . . . . . . . . . . . *63*
Question 121. . . . . . . . . . . . . . . . . . *63*
Question 124. . . . . . . . . . . . . . . . . . *65*
Question 128. . . . . . . . . . . . . . . . . . *67*
Question 136. . . . . . . . . . . . . . . . . . *72*
Question 138. . . . . . . . . . . . . . . . . . *73*
Question 149. . . . . . . . . . . . . . . . . . *79*
Question 156. . . . . . . . . . . . . . . . . . *82*
Question 160. . . . . . . . . . . . . . . . . . *84*
Question 166. . . . . . . . . . . . . . . . . . *87*
Question 168. . . . . . . . . . . . . . . . . . *88*
Question 169. . . . . . . . . . . . . . . . . . *89*
Question 171. . . . . . . . . . . . . . . . . . *90*
Question 181. . . . . . . . . . . . . . . . . . *95*
Question 196. . . . . . . . . . . . . . . . . . *102*
Question 197. . . . . . . . . . . . . . . . . . *103*
Question 198. . . . . . . . . . . . . . . . . . *103*
Question 199. . . . . . . . . . . . . . . . . . *104*

## Monitoring & Controlling

|  | Page |
|---|---|
| Question 26 | 16 |
| Question 36 | 22 |
| Question 48 | 29 |
| Question 49 | 29 |
| Question 50 | 30 |
| Question 52 | 31 |
| Question 56 | 33 |
| Question 58 | 33 |
| Question 61 | 35 |
| Question 64 | 37 |
| Question 81 | 45 |
| Question 87 | 48 |
| Question 92 | 50 |
| Question 95 | 52 |
| Question 111 | 59 |
| Question 112 | 60 |
| Question 113 | 60 |
| Question 122 | 64 |
| Question 123 | 64 |
| Question 126 | 66 |
| Question 127 | 66 |
| Question 133 | 70 |
| Question 134 | 70 |
| Question 135 | 71 |
| Question 139 | 74 |

Question 141. . . . . . . . . . . . . . . . . *75*
Question 143. . . . . . . . . . . . . . . . . *76*
Question 148. . . . . . . . . . . . . . . . . *78*
Question 150. . . . . . . . . . . . . . . . . *79*
Question 151. . . . . . . . . . . . . . . . . *80*
Question 155. . . . . . . . . . . . . . . . . *82*
Question 162. . . . . . . . . . . . . . . . . *85*
Question 163. . . . . . . . . . . . . . . . . *85*
Question 165. . . . . . . . . . . . . . . . . *86*
Question 167. . . . . . . . . . . . . . . . . *87*
Question 172. . . . . . . . . . . . . . . . . *90*
Question 175. . . . . . . . . . . . . . . . . *92*
Question 179. . . . . . . . . . . . . . . . . *94*
Question 180. . . . . . . . . . . . . . . . . *94*
Question 184. . . . . . . . . . . . . . . . . *96*
Question 192. . . . . . . . . . . . . . . . . *100*
Question 195. . . . . . . . . . . . . . . . . *102*

## Closing

|  | Page |
|---|---|
| Question 4. . . . . . . . . . . . . . . . . . . . .4 | |
| Question 5. . . . . . . . . . . . . . . . . . . . .4 | |
| Question 22. . . . . . . . . . . . . . . . . .14 | |
| Question 30. . . . . . . . . . . . . . . . . .18 | |
| Question 60. . . . . . . . . . . . . . . . . .34 | |
| Question 75. . . . . . . . . . . . . . . . . .42 | |
| Question 103. . . . . . . . . . . . . . . . .56 | |
| Question 129. . . . . . . . . . . . . . . . .68 | |
| Question 130. . . . . . . . . . . . . . . . .68 | |
| Question 142. . . . . . . . . . . . . . . . .75 | |
| Question 157. . . . . . . . . . . . . . . . .83 | |
| Question 158. . . . . . . . . . . . . . . . .83 | |
| Question 182. . . . . . . . . . . . . . . . .95 | |
| Question 183. . . . . . . . . . . . . . . . .96 | |
| Question 186. . . . . . . . . . . . . . . . .97 | |
| Question 187. . . . . . . . . . . . . . . . .98 | |
| Question 188. . . . . . . . . . . . . . . . .98 | |
| Question 191. . . . . . . . . . . . . . . .100 | |

## Professional Responsibility

| | Page |
|---|---|
| Question 2 | 2 |
| Question 11 | 8 |
| Question 19 | 13 |
| Question 35 | 22 |
| Question 43 | 26 |
| Question 84 | 46 |
| Question 100 | 54 |
| Question 140 | 74 |
| Question 144 | 76 |
| Question 146 | 77 |
| Question 159 | 83 |
| Question 161 | 84 |
| Question 176 | 92 |
| Question 178 | 93 |
| Question 185 | 97 |
| Question 189 | 99 |
| Question 190 | 99 |
| Question 193 | 101 |